Grow Organic

A SIMPLE GUIDE TO NOVA SCOTIA VEGETABLE GARDENING

by Elizabeth Peirce

NIMBUS
PUBLISHING

For Elsie, Martha, and Sophie-Tang—
past, present, and future gardeners.

Nimbus Publishing Limited
PO Box 9166, Halifax, NS B3K 5M8
(902) 455-4286
www.nimbus.ca

Design and illustration: Margaret Issenman

Printed and bound in Canada

Library and Archives Canada Cataloguing in Publication

Peirce, Elizabeth, 1975-

Grow organic : a simple guide to Nova Scotia vegetable gardening / Elizabeth Peirce.

Includes bibliographical references and index.

ISBN 978-1-55109-750-3

1. Vegetable gardening—Nova Scotia. 2. Organic gardening—Nova Scotia.

I. Title.

SB324.3.P425 2010   635'.09716   C2009-907274-2

We acknowledge the financial support of the Government of Canada through the Book Publishing Industry Development Program (BPIDP) and the Canada Council, and of the Province of Nova Scotia through the Department of Tourism, Culture and Heritage for our publishing activities.

Mixed Sources
Product group from well-managed forests and other controlled sources
www.fsc.org Cert no. SW-COC-000952
© 1996 Forest Stewardship Council

Contents

Preface

An enthusiastic amateur gardener, I have been involved in the growing and preserving of vegetables for the last thirty years and am always eager to hear about others' gardening enterprises, in book form or in person. I should preface my remarks by saying that I attempt to use only organic methods in the food that I grow; I don't use pesticides.

There are few hard and fast rules when it comes to growing vegetables, but there are some things you can do to make the process a bit easier.

Where my own knowledge of a topic is limited, I have consulted others—in person, on the Internet, and in the many garden books out there. Because this is meant to be a beginner's guide rather than a detailed garden manual, not all subjects may get the attention they deserve; if your interest is piqued, please check the bibliography at the back of the book for more information. I've also included the stories of some local urban gardeners who I hope will inspire more folks to view growing food in the city as a normal part of a sustainable urban lifestyle. Happy reading—and even happier gardening!

The author helps her grandmother with the potato harvest in 1978.

Acknowledgements

With thanks to the farmers and orchardists of Nova Scotia, who keep the faith; Penelope Jackson for her good idea; Patrick Murphy; Paula Sarson for her excellent editing; David McLearn for introducing me to veggie landscaping; Jean Snow and Bob Kropla, whose yard feeds many; Michelle Smith and her tomatoes; Janet and Hudson Shotwell and their inspiring garden party; Susan Kerslake and her balcony; Jayme Melrose; Owen and Colin Bridge and their scythes; Sebastian Margarit and his artichokes; Joanna Brown and the women of the Spryfield Urban Farm Museum; Faythe Buchanan; Sandra Barry and the Elizabeth Bishop House, where one can write in peace and comfort; Clare Goulet and Graham Fraser for their friendship; Ruth Whitehead; the Brunswick Street crew; Noel and Ted Guppy; Janet Baker; and Ian Guppy, fellow forager, with love.

Introduction

Gardeners are the world's greatest optimists, and well-versed in a variety of fields, from meteorology to soil ecology, entomology to landscaping. Perhaps more than the average person, gardeners, especially those who grow at least a portion of their own food, are worried about the effects of climate change—they keep a watchful eye on weather patterns, often recording changes from year to year in their journals.

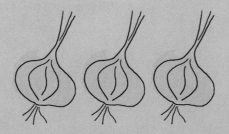

Nova Scotia has a long and proud history of gardening on both a large and small scale: the first European inhabitants of the province grew French-style gardens at Port Royal in the first decade of the 1600s, while those who followed them—the Acadians, the Planters, and the Black Loyalists, among others—worked the land on a larger scale, building *aboiteaux*, planting orchards, growing grain and vegetables for their own use and to sell at market. Our ancestors led lives that were dictated by seasonal necessity: on the North Shore, where I've spent summers gardening since I was a small child, men and women worked the fishing season harvesting and canning lobster; when the season

Kale and chard aplenty! These hardy greens will keep growing well into the colder days of fall.

ended in late June, they turned their attentions to putting in the garden. To gardeners in the Annapolis Valley, where folks would be enjoying their peas and spinach on Canada Day, this would have seemed like a very late start, but Nova Scotia's geography and climate are varied. You can see it in the trees in spring; the leaves come out much later on the North Shore than in Halifax, which, in turn, lags well behind the Valley.

My own family history has its roots in the rich soil of the Annapolis Valley, where my mother's people are from. Many of my maternal ancestors were orchardists or subsistence farmers, deeply connected to the land. I consider my grandparents farmers, though they had to leave the Valley when my grandfather began working in the bank. As a girl growing up in Truro in the 1950s, my mother remembers late summer visits "home," a place she had never lived in but with which she maintained a spiritual connection, where the sheer abundance and fertility of the landscape and the generosity of its people made a profound impression. A visit to Aunt Mabel's meant a visit to the garden, where a ripe cushion-sized tomato and an armload of corn, shucked at the back door, made up supper. Cousins and friends could be counted on to slip a bushel of apples, a box of raspberries grown on backyard canes, or a squash bigger than an adult's head into the trunk. My grandmother would sometimes be embarrassed by how much produce they invariably brought back to Truro after such visits; "They'll think we're looking for handouts," she'd worry.

I find the generosity of gardeners, not just towards their relatives but also to anyone who shows an interest in their garden, a wonderful thing. It's not just the vegetables that they are willing to share, but perhaps more inspiring and helpful still, their hard-earned knowledge. I treasure it.

In an age when soaring energy prices have dramatically increased the price of food, especially fresh vegetables, by as much as 25 percent, people are turning to gardens in ways we might not have imagined. Just a few months before the fall of 2008, when the world financial system foundered, a newspaper article reported that the British government was contemplating asking its citizens to plant "victory gardens" as they did during the food-rationing period during and after World War II. Meanwhile, in the United States, garden centres are reporting record sales of vegetable seed, as soaring oil prices keep more and more North Americans at home on their vacations. For the first time in decades, vegetables have overtaken annual flowers in popularity among gardeners, second only to lawn maintenance on North Americans' list of landscaping priorities. If food prices continue to increase, as they seem sure to, one wonders if—

hopes that—more of those lawns will be turned over to the cultivation of food.

With more and more questions surfacing about the safety of the foods we eat, many of them mass produced, the need to know where our food is grown and under what conditions has also never been stronger; witness the amazing growth in popularity of farmers' markets in our province and elsewhere. For the first time in decades, first-time gardeners are pouring into garden centres, looking for advice on growing their own vegetables. These novices—many of them urban and twenty-something—are motivated, perhaps, by a perfect storm of global recession, food safety concerns, and a new environmentalism that wants to know why those snow peas and that garlic were flown in from Asia when they could have been grown right here in Nova Scotia.

On a bus ride to the suburbs to visit a friend's garden recently, I saw an inspiring sight: the front lawn of a fifties-style suburban dwelling under full cultivation. Potatoes, beans, and carrots were well underway. As the bus lingered at a stoplight, I was struck by the rarity of this sight and wished suddenly that it were not so rare. It is my hope that more city and suburb dwellers become acquainted with the enormous satisfaction found in producing and preserving our own food, or at least the benefits of buying and eating local food, whether grown by us or by those near us.

The Baker family's Victory Garden, summer 1944

CHAPTER 1

Beyond the Lawn: Some Preliminaries

First-time gardeners are faced with a number of questions and decisions before their trowels ever touch the soil. Here is a breakdown of everything you need to think about before you start digging.

Where should I put my garden?

Plants need ample amounts of sunlight to grow and flourish—at the very least, two to six hours of sunlight per day. You can control some sources of shade in your garden space by sacrificing an ornamental shrub or two or by positioning your garden so it receives the best possible (southern) exposure, but some shade sources are beyond your control, like the tall building or leafy tree next door. If you have inherited a backyard with a permanent shade problem, you may have to get creative with your space: how sunny is your front lawn, for example? If there are already flower beds out front, how would you feel about slipping a few veggies in there? Gardens don't need to be conventional, and many flowers and vegetables are well-suited companions in the garden.

Here's a bit of good news for those gardeners not blessed with full unimpeded sunlight on their property. Many vegetables and herbs can be grown in a partially shaded location (though no plant can grow in total shade). As mentioned before, two to six hours of direct sunlight per day is considered the minimum. Plants grown in partial shade may not be as prolific as their full-sun counterparts, but will still yield a moderate harvest.

If you have both full sun and partial-shade garden space available, it's a good idea to reserve the full-sun location for heat-loving crops like tomatoes, peppers, and basil.

Edible nasturtiums (the lily pad-leafed flower) share space with leafy greens in this raised bed.

What should I grow?

Deciding what to grow in a home garden can be daunting: looking through seed catalogues with hundreds of varieties of vegetables doesn't help narrow things down at all.

Some choices should be easy: for instance, if you don't have much space, you may have to abandon your dream of growing and milling your own wheat. If you're from the Maritimes, you can also pretty well give up on growing things like okra, peanuts, and most kinds of melons, unless and until global warming makes our eastern Canadian growing seasons longer and hotter.

Nevertheless, your choice of vegetables for your home garden is quite broad, and with a little planning, you can enjoy a selection of fresh produce all through the summer months and well into the fall.

So what should you plant?

Much will depend on your own preferences and those of the people who will share in your harvest. In the following chapters, I'll introduce you to some vegetables that grow well in our fairly brief Maritime summer, along with tips for preserving them, should you choose to.

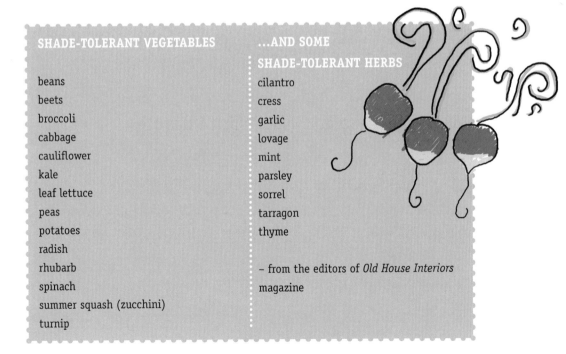

SHADE-TOLERANT VEGETABLES

beans
beets
broccoli
cabbage
cauliflower
kale
leaf lettuce
peas
potatoes
radish
rhubarb
spinach
summer squash (zucchini)
turnip

**...AND SOME
SHADE-TOLERANT HERBS**

cilantro
cress
garlic
lovage
mint
parsley
sorrel
tarragon
thyme

– from the editors of *Old House Interiors*
magazine

How much space do I have?

Tied in with location, your space may be limited by external factors, such as the size of your lot, or by individual factors, such as your family's or pets' need for lawn space, or competition from flower beds.

Are your vegetables just for summer eating, or do you also want to put some away for winter? If the latter, you'll want to allow space for winter root crops as well as veggies that can be turned into preserves—tomatoes and cucumbers.

Scarlet Runner beans climb strings on Susan Kerslake's Halifax balcony.

The size of the plant you want to grow when it reaches maturity is another factor to consider, especially for balcony gardeners and others who don't have much space: members of the squash family, in particular, can quickly take over a small garden patch.

There are solutions to a space crunch. Some plants—cucumbers, beans, squash—can be trellised up or otherwise encouraged to grow vertically; others, like cherry tomatoes, strawberries, and herbs will happily live in hanging baskets.

How much time and effort can I devote to the garden?

If you answered "not so much," it doesn't make you a bad person. You may not end up with the most aesthetically pleasing garden, but vegetables will still grow even when you're away on vacation. First-timers should start small to gauge their level of enthusiasm for the project.

Should I use seeds or transplants?

Impatient gardeners may want to buy transplants from a garden centre or farmers' market. Transplants have an obvious head start on seeds and will get you eating from the garden a lot sooner, though they are more expensive than seed.

Many seasoned gardeners prefer to save their own seed—and save money in the process (see page 13 for more on how to do this, or consult one of the many guides to seed saving, such as Carole Turner's *Seed Sowing and Saving*). You can also start your seeds inside early and then transplant them later: this works especially well with tomatoes and squash. You'll want to time things right so the transplants go into the garden when they're somewhere between tiny and fragile and tall, leggy, and reaching for the light. Start your seeds about eight weeks before the time you plant them out: for information about frost dates and when to start transplanting, see page 16.

If you've acquired your seeds a bit in advance, have a sunny window and some extra time, why not give your seeds a jump start on life? Many vegetables can successfully be started indoors for later transplanting, such as tomatoes, peppers, cabbage, broccoli, and kale.

In spring, your sunny window ledge can be turned into a hothouse for tomato seedlings.

A NOTE ON PEAT

Peat moss is a common potting medium and soil conditioner. Its spongy, porous consistency helps to lighten up heavy clay soil, though it doesn't add nutrients and often blows away if left on the surface of the soil, necessitating repeated applications.

Peat comes from natural bogs, and its removal damages the sensitive ecosystem in the bog, which took thousands of years to develop. For that reason, some gardeners prefer to use more sustainable soil amendments, such as leaf meal, compost, or coconut fibre in their gardens, which improve both the consistency and the nutrient value of the soil.

You'll hear a lot about heirloom plant varieties these days, but what are they? Usually the term "heirloom" means an open-pollinated (non-hybrid) variety that was first introduced more than fifty years ago, but which is now rarely available in most seed catalogues. (Open-pollinated means pollinated by wind, insects, birds, or animals rather than by human intervention. By contrast, hybrids are propagated by human methods such as cutting or division.) These almost-forgotten old varieties have survived thanks to the efforts of individual gardeners who appreciated their qualities, grew the plants out from year to year and saved the seed, keeping the strain from crossing with other varieties. Many of these old strains are vigorous and well-adapted to the climate where they were grown, making them less susceptible to diseases and pests than their inbred hybrid cousins. Heirloom seeds have been exchanged among gardeners informally for years, but sometimes, more organized seed exchanges have emerged on the scene, such as the Canadian seed-saving organization Seeds of Diversity.

Most garden centres and some seed companies carry small, disk-like peat pellets that expand when you add water to them; one seed can be added to each pot (don't bury it too deeply). If you want to save some money, you can buy a bag of potting mix and make your own pots: old coffee cups (paper or Styrofoam), the bottom half of milk cartons, yogourt containers, or recycled plastic plant pots are all good choices (make sure they're clean!). You will need to poke a few drainage holes in your container and place it on a plate or tray so it doesn't drip when you water it.

Your seeds need light and damp soil in order to sprout: make sure you put your pots in a sunny window and don't forget to water them regularly when you notice the soil is dry. If you don't get a lot of natural light in your house or apartment, you can set the pots on a table under a fluorescent shop light.

When your seedlings are a few inches high, it's time to plant them. It's a good idea to "harden off" your seedlings, that is, give them a taste of the great outdoors prior to actually planting them (although this part is not strictly necessary in most cases). Pick a relatively warm day for this, and leave the seedlings out for a few hours, bringing them in at night when it's cold. Repeat for a few days, and then plant them.

Where should I get my seeds?

Many seed companies (Veseys, Halifax Seed, William Dam Seeds Ltd, Johnny's) offer a wide selection of vegetable varieties, including the latest hybrids, and will send you a free catalogue upon request. These colourful catalogues, packed with tempting descriptions of each vegetable's best features, are delicious reading for gardeners on long winter evenings.

In the spring, your local grocery or hardware store will usually carry a shelf of the most popular seed varieties for a couple of dollars per package. Some even carry a line of organically grown seed (look for the "Organics" label at the Atlantic Superstore).

If you are concerned about buying genetically modified seed, you should check the catalogue to see if the company has taken the "Safe Seed Pledge," which states that the company has not knowingly bought or sold genetically engineered seeds. You can also contact the company directly and ask about their suppliers and their policies.

Do-it-yourself: Seeds of Diversity

Environmentally committed gardeners who are concerned about the rapidly decreasing genetic diversity of seed as more and more old varieties are no longer sold commercially should consider becoming members of the national charitable organization Seeds of Diversity whose mandate is "to ensure food security and abundant choices by engaging Canadians to live the tradition of using and conserving endangered and heritage plants." An annual thirty-dollar membership fee puts you in a nation-wide loop of heritage seed growers willing to share their stock with you. (You pay the postage: some growers accept Canadian Tire money and postage stamps for this purpose!) The annual seed exchange directory put out by SoD includes, among other delights, well over five hundred varieties of heirloom tomatoes with fantastic names like "Mortgage Lifter," "Teton de Venus," and "Abraham Lincoln."

Rather than using its seed-exchange directory as a seed catalogue, SoD encourages members to grow out and save their own seed; this will help to assure that variety's survival, should other stocks fail.

Note: Not all vegetables are created equal and some varieties will get crossed up if planted too close together (this is especially true of the squash family). To help you sort it all out, SoD offers handbooks on seed saving for beginners. Contact them at seeds.ca.

Two Maritime heirloom seed companies

If you don't have the time and energy to commit to seed saving but like the idea of using old varieties, you can always buy heritage seeds. Here are a couple of local options. It's a good idea to order early in the spring to avoid the disappointment of seed shortages—remember that these are small companies that produce a limited amount of seed each year.

Hope Seeds

PO Box 130, Glassville, NB E7L 4T4

hopeseed.com

Hope Seeds offers certified organic, open-pollinated varieties of veggies, herbs, Jerusalem artichokes, and seed potatoes. Their "mix-and-match" grab-bag of potato varieties is a fantastic idea; with all of those good-looking spuds, how can you choose among them?

Annapolis Seeds

8528 Hwy 201, RR3, Middleton, NS B0S 1P0

annapolisseeds.com

This is a fledgling Nova Scotian seed company run by the amazing seventeen-year-old Owen Bridge (recently profiled in *Rural Delivery* magazine). Bridge is committed to sustainable, organic agriculture. His seed is organically grown and GM-free, and he encourages others to save their own seed. (For more information on Owen Bridge, see page 123.)

Some of Annapolis Seeds' stock awaiting packaging

Other Canadian heirloom companies

Write or email them for a free catalogue.

Heritage Harvest Seed

Box 40, RR3, Carman, MB R0G 0J0

Phone: 204-745-6489

heritageharvestseed.com

Organically grown seed (though not certified organic). Four hundred varieties of heirloom veggies (one hundred heritage tomatoes), flowers, and herbs.

Terra Edibles

535 Ashley Street, Foxboro, ON K0K 2B0

Phone: 613-961-0654

terraedibles.ca

Certified organic seed. Eighty heirloom tomato varieties, plus veggies, herbs, and flowers.

Seed tips for the first-time gardener

1. Share a seed order with a friend; first-time gardeners are notorious over-orderers. You can share costs and seed with a friend or gardening neighbour. Most leftover seed can be kept fresh in the freezer; I put them in plastic film canisters inside a Ziploc or other plastic bag. Or, you can give extra seed to your local community garden.
2. It's always a good idea to use catalogues that stock seed designed with your growing area in mind; reserve those California catalogues for fantasy reading.
3. Make your own compost, the cheapest and most sustainable kind of fertilizer (see Chapter 2 for instructions).
4. Use mulch during a hot—or any—summer: it keeps weeds down and moisture in the soil it covers (see Chapter 2 for more information). A little extra time spent mulching at the beginning of the season will really pay off in the heat of summer, prime weed time.

A note on seed saving for all vegetables

In the following chapters, you'll find tips on saving seeds for many different kinds of vegetables. It's important to note that not all vegetables make good candidates for seed-saving since not all plants are pollinated the same way and many will cross-pollinate if you or your neighbours are growing different varieties of the same vegetable. This is often the case in urban community garden settings where vegetable patches are spaced quite closely together. (The term "pollination" refers to "the transfer of pollen from an anther to a stigma, either on the same flower or from one flower to another. Pollination leads to fertilization and production of seeds." Turner, *Seed Sowing and Saving*, 211.) In the descriptions of individual vegetables that follow, you'll find a note on how that vegetable is pollinated—some do it themselves, some are pollinated by wind or by insects—and which ones produce seeds that will breed true the following year.

How soon can I begin planting?

You'll hear a lot about frost dates in spring and fall if you spend time with gardeners; these are the dates before (spring) and after (fall) which there is a danger of a plant-killing frost. Frost dates vary by location or "zone." Most of Nova Scotia is in Zone 5, though the southern portion is in Zone 6. (Zones are determined by the range of average annual minimum temperatures: Zone 5 ranges from −29 to −23 °C (−20 to −10°F) while Zone 6 ranges from −23 to −18 °C (−10 to 0 °F). Even in a province as small as ours, there is considerable variation in last frost dates; in Yarmouth, for example, that date is May 1, while in Sydney, it is May 24.

Many Nova Scotia gardeners will tell you that it is safe to plant your garden around the time when the lilacs and apples bloom; the days may be warm, but frost still can hit on our cold early-May nights.

It's a good idea to listen to your local weather forecasts in late September and early October for heavy frost warnings—the majority of your crops should be harvested and brought indoors before the nights start to get really cold (although some vegetables, like carrots, parsnips, and especially kale, don't mind the cold and will actually improve in flavour after being nipped by the frost).

Ways to warm the soil

If you're really anxious to get started, cover your garden space with clear plastic for two or three weeks before planting time—this can really raise the soil temperature. So can floating row cover spread over the patch. Digging or tilling the soil will also help warm it up, though not as quickly. Raised beds have an early season advantage over conventional gardens in warming up more quickly.

What tools will I need?

Buy or borrow these basic gardening tools—catalogues such as Johnny's Seed, Lee Valley, and others will carry dozens of variations on the theme, but these are ones you shouldn't be without:

- A good shovel (for hand-turning the soil, digging potatoes)
- A hoe (for weeding and sowing—keep a good, sharp edge on it)
- A garden rake (for levelling out turned soil in preparation for sowing—not the kind used for raking leaves)
- A trowel (great for digging holes for transplants and spot-weeding)

You may need to rent a tiller if you're planning to dig up a portion of your lawn and don't relish doing it the old-fashioned way with a shovel. See page 31 for information on the pros and cons of tilling.

Cleaning your tools

Keep a bucket of sand with linseed oil poured into it in your garage or basement for dipping your trowel and hoe blade in after you've used them—the sand will scour off the dirt and your tool will get oiled at the same time.

Do I need to keep a record of what I plant?

It's a great idea to keep a garden journal. Making a rough map of your garden in a specially designated journal will help you to remember what grew where each year. A journal is also a good place to jot down each season's significant events in the life of your garden. Was it a wet or dry summer? Were any crops the victims of an insect infestation, and what did you do about it? On what date did the first tomato/bean/spinach leaf appear and on what date did you enjoy a good meal of each crop? It's always fun to read journal entries in the dead of winter and to write down plans for the next season there.

Crop rotation

Keeping a garden journal will also help you rotate your crops. Because different vegetables draw different levels of nutrients from the soil, it is important not to plant vegetables from the same family in the same place year after year. Rotating crops will ensure that you are not depleting your soil, that vegetables are getting adequate nutrients, and that veggie-specific pests and diseases do not get a toehold in the ground. If you use raised beds, you can plant vegetables from the same family in one bed the first year, then in a different bed in the second year.

The author's North Shore garden, ready for the harvest

How should I water my garden?

Many experienced gardeners will tell you that the only watering their vegetables get during the summer is a good old-fashioned drenching from Mother Nature now and then. Many of us underestimate the amount of water it takes to reach down to the roots of a quickly growing plant—shallow watering can actually do more harm than no watering at all since thirsty roots will turn upwards to reach the moisture rather than burrow downwards towards the moist subsoil and thus risk drying out, killing the plant.

If you choose to give your garden an occasional good soaking, storing rainwater makes sense, especially if you want to mix up a batch of compost tea to fertilize your tomatoes and cucumbers. It takes only a few hours of steady rain to fill most rain barrels to overflowing.

If your house is on a hill with the garden at the bottom of the slope, you can use a drip irrigation hose (basically, a regular hose with many holes drilled along its whole length) connected to your barrel or succession of barrels, and let gravity do your work for you. If your rain barrel has a spigot attached, you can easily fill your watering can (you'll need to make several trips), or you can simply dip the water out from the top of the barrel. Be aware that standing water breeds mosquitoes, so try to get a rain barrel with a lid.

Some rain barrels can be connected with a spill-over hose to maximize rainwater storage from a single drainspout.

You can use just about any kind of watertight receptacle to collect your rainwater. If you'd rather buy one, Lee Valley makes a really neat collapsible vinyl rain barrel that holds up to 400 litres (105 U.S. gallons), for around a hundred dollars. If you prefer a more traditional wooden barrel with metal hoops, check out Richard Countway Silviculture Ltd. (novascotiabarrels.blogspot.com) of Chester Basin, Nova Scotia—a place once known as the barrel capital of Canada. A large poplar barrel costs about seventy-five dollars. For information on buying one of these fine barrels in Halifax, call 880-0398.

A few final words of caution before you get started

Don't plant all your seed at once. If there's a drought or a period of constant, heavy rain, you may need to replant, and if you've ordered by catalogue, many varieties will be sold out by the time you're ready to start again.

Be realistic about what varieties to plant. Our neighbour, who hailed from Alabama, had a hankering for homegrown okra, but its long maturation period and Nova Scotia's relatively short growing season were not a good fit. Other warm-weather vegetables that have broken my heart over the years include eggplant (I can get them to walnut size, but no larger), cantaloupe (one Arctic variety did well one exceptionally good year, but failed the other five years we tried), and peanuts (leave them to Georgia).

Don't plant more than you can tend. You can always give extra produce away to friends or to the food bank, but if you neglect your plot and let the weeds take it over you won't have much of anything, even for yourself. A small, well-tended garden is better than a large neglected one.

You've ordered your seeds and they're on their way. You've bought or borrowed the tools you'll need. You've chosen the perfect spot in your yard. Now it's time to look at the soil your seeds will be growing in.

CHAPTER 2

Work With What You Have: Soil 101

Once you've picked a spot for your garden, it's time to think about the condition of the soil. Is it healthy and nutrient-rich enough to meet the demands of growing plants that will soon be feeding you?

Preparing the soil

Organic gardeners agree that the best thing you can do for your soil is to give it big, regular helpings of compost. Compost expert Grace Gershuny writes, "Composting is the art and science of mixing various organic materials in a pile and controlling the conditions so that soil organisms break down the raw organic matter into humus. It mimics the natural humus-formation processes that take place whenever leaves fall or plants die." (*Healthy Soils for Sustainable Gardens,* 51.) Also known as "black gold," this wondrously fertile material is teeming with microbial life that helps plants grow and fight off diseases. Earthworms chew through the raw materials, breaking them down, and excrete nutrient-rich castings which further enrich the soil.

Compost greatly improves the condition of all types of soil, from heavy clay to sandy soil, and helps restore balance to soils deficient in one of the three main nutrients plants need to grow: nitrogen (N), phosphorus (P), and potassium (K) (these are the nutrients represented by the three numbers you see on bags of fertilizer at garden centres). Compost is nature's gift to us.

Finished compost has the texture of coffee grounds.

The wonderful thing about compost is that you can make your own at home and it doesn't cost a penny. Garden centres sell many varieties of home composters, from wooden-slatted square bins to black plastic tumblers, but the truth is, you can start a compost pile anywhere. (The only reason for the containers is aesthetic—some people don't like the look of a compost pile.) If you live in a municipality that collects compost and processes it at a central location, you may want to rethink giving away your kitchen scraps and yard waste: these are the cornerstones of home composting. The reams of literature on composting will tell you about the importance of maintaining a carbon ("browns") and nitrogen ("greens") balance in your heap: some compost

A mixture of leaves and food scraps is a good basic recipe for compost.

WHAT COUNTS AS CARBON?	WHAT COUNTS AS NITROGEN?
corn cobs and stalks	animal manure (don't use cat or dog
dryer lint (best from natural fibres)	feces, which can contain harmful
leaves	pathogens)
newspaper (don't use the coloured	coffee grounds
pages or glossy inserts: they contain	fruit and vegetable peelings
chemicals)	grass clippings
pine needles	green comfrey leaves (great compost
sawdust (from untreated lumber)	activator)
shrub prunings	lawn and garden weeds
straw or hay	tea leaves
wood ash	
wood chips	

aficionados will tell you that the proper carbon-nitrogen ratio is around 30:1, while others say it is about half-and-half. Don't concern yourself too much about the numbers; everything will break down eventually. I've found, though, that putting too many kitchen scraps ("greens") in my bin at once made for a soggy, anaerobic mess that smelled bad. Once I started adding leaves and straw to the mix and covered my bin against the wet Maritime weather, things improved.

Rates of decomposition of organic materials will vary. The best thing you can do to speed up the process is to chop your kitchen scraps into small chunks and mow over your dead leaves with a power mower (leaves are notoriously slow decomposers since they tend to mat on your pile).

Another way to speed up the composting process is to turn your pile regularly. Using a garden fork, dig into the pile, bringing the bottom layers up to the top and "fluffing" the likely compacted vegetable matter so that the air can get at it. This may be a stinky job if your pile is wet and the "greens" have turned anaerobic; it's a good idea to keep a pile of leaves or other "brown" materials near your pile to throw on top of smellier kitchen scraps.

Other materials that feed the soil

So it's your first year of gardening and you don't have time to wait for the microbes to work their magic on your kitchen scraps in the new compost heap. Or maybe you're planning a garden for next season and are looking for ways to build up your soil. Here are some suggestions:

1. Cover crops/green manure

A great way to add fertility to poor or exhausted soil is to plant a cool-season cover crop (also known as green manure) during the times when your garden space is not being used to grow vegetables. Many garden centres carry buckwheat, winter rye, vetch, or pea seed in bulk, all of which can be broadcast sown (i.e., thrown by the handful) on the soil and left to do its thing until the frost kills it or until you till it under; this practice adds valuable nutrients to the soil which are used by other crops.

A 23-kilogram (50-pound) bag of cheap birdseed is a good way to feed your garden. It usually contains sunflowers, millet, and other seeds that will make excellent green manure when thickly sown in your garden. (Don't worry about covering the seed with soil—think of all the seeds in nature that don't get covered and still grow!) Birdseed is a good source of nitrogen in the compost heap as well.

2. Seaweed

We are blessed with an abundance of seaweed here in the Maritimes; if you are lucky enough to live near a beach, you can collect it for free (or find a friend with a seaside cottage who can gather up some for you). Seaweed, along with other algae, is one of the best possible soil amendments around—the microbes in your soil love it. You can add the seaweed directly to your compost pile. (Try for the stuff that's been washed up high on the beach since most of the salt will have washed out of it. You can rinse your seaweed out at home with the hose, just to be sure.) Leave a clump of seaweed to soak in a bucket of fresh water for a couple of days to make a tea that you can water plants with.

3. Grass clippings

These are very high in nitrogen. Like seaweed, they can be soaked in water to make a foliar tea or used directly on the garden as a mulch or side dressing for plants.

4. Wood ashes

Containing up to 70 percent calcium carbonate and lots of potassium, these are great, especially for our slightly acidic Maritime soils, since ashes are alkaline. Ashes are also good sprinkled into your compost pile. Be sure to use wood ashes only, not charcoal or coloured-paper ashes, which contain chemicals.

5. Animal manure

An excellent source of three main plant nutrients (N, P, and K), manure needs to be well composted before adding to the garden since the fresh stuff is very strong and may burn your plants' roots. To be on the safe side, go with the manure of vegetarian animals like cows and horses. Well-composted chicken manure is also great; sweet peas love it!

6. "Fast Food": dry dog or cat food/pond fish feed

A purist might not call these truly organic soil amendments, but their high protein content (most contain fish meal) makes them a good choice as a side dressing for heavy feeders like squash, or you can soak smaller amounts of them in water to make a compost tea for watering.

A NOTE ON BIOSOLIDS

With the recent arrival of sewage treatment in the Halifax Regional Municipality, a debate over the use of biosolids on agricultural land has arisen. (Biosolids is the term used to describe sewage sludge mixed with cement kiln dust to create a fertilizer.) While there is no doubt that human waste contains valuable nutrients, it also contains an unknown combination of drug residues, heavy metals, cleaning products, flame retardants, and whatever else gets flushed down city toilets, none of it currently filtered out at our local sewage treatment plants.

Organic growers currently are not allowed to use biosolids on their soil. If you have concerns, it would seem wise to apply the precautionary principle and not use this material on your food crops either.

Mulch away!

Mulch is "vegetable matter spread around or over a plant to enrich or insulate the soil or suppress weeds" (*The Paperback Canadian Oxford Dictionary*). Whatever mulching material you choose (read on for some suggestions), a few minutes spent mulching at the beginning of the growing season can really save a lot of time and effort later on when weeds are in full swing.

Leaves: the free, all-purpose mulch

If you have deciduous (leaf-bearing) trees on your property, don't throw the leaves out on garbage day in the fall or spring! Add them directly to your compost heap to provide a carbon balance for your nitrogen-rich kitchen scraps.

Leaves make wonderful mulch. Run your lawnmower over them to shred them into more quickly compostable leaf meal, which can be applied around the base of seedlings to keep down weeds and keep in moisture. The urban treeless can usually pick up extra bags of discarded leaves in the fall and spring when people are tidying their lawns.

Fall is a great time to stock up on mulching material.

Other kinds of mulch

Old hay or straw, rotted sawdust, seaweed, eel grass, pine needles, unsprayed grass clippings, and shredded bark can all be used as mulch, although wood-based mulches take longer to break down than other materials and so may not be ideal for a one-season vegetable garden. Use chunkier mulches like bark for perennials instead.

Soil tests for a dirty world

The Canadian Council of Ministers of the Environment's *Canadian Soil Quality Guidelines* recommends levels of lead no higher than 70 mg/kg—or parts per million—for agricultural lands. (Residential or park land should have levels of lead no higher than 140 mg/kg). It seems that the Canadian guidelines for lead are more stringent than in other places; the University of Minnesota Extension Service website tells us that vegetables grown in garden soil with lead levels of up to 300 mg/kg can be eaten safely. The main concern with soil containing this much lead would be the potential for direct ingestion by small children.

For a number of reasons, it is a good idea to have the soil in your yard tested before you start growing your food in it; this test will give you important information about the composition of your garden soil and clues to what your predecessors might have used that space for—beloved garden patch or garbage dump.

Lead

Sadly, we live in a world contaminated by all sorts of pollutants, some of which may be lurking in your backyard. Of particular concern to urban gardeners, especially those with children, is lead, a heavy metal once commonly found in house paints and gasoline. Though paint and gas manufacturers have long since removed lead from their products, the metal can remain in the soil for years, some of it being absorbed by your vegetables, and ultimately, by you. "Chronic exposure to heavy metals—either by direct contact or by eating produce grown in contaminated soil—can damage your nervous system and major organs" (*Healthy Soils for Sustainable Gardens* 96). If you're planting your garden near an older building or a busy roadway, you may want to consider having your soil tested for lead, the most common heavy metal contaminant of soil.

Contact a lab that does heavy-metal testing to find out what kind of container they prefer for soil samples (most will provide you with one). It's best not to use a metal implement for soil collecting, as this might affect the results.

It's common for lead to be found at varying levels in different parts of your yard. Consider bringing in a sample from each area and be sure to label your specimens accurately.

If your test reveals lead in your soil sample, there are a few things you can do:

1. Low-level lead-contaminated soil benefits from added compost and mulch; these materials bind up contaminants, making them less available to plants. Other non-harmful soil additives that reduce the bioavailability of lead are lime and clay.

2. Certain plants can be used as soil cleansers. Spinach, sunflowers, and members of the mustard family will absorb lead from the soil, though possibly not in great amounts. If you've grown these plants specifically to act as lead-absorbers in a known high-lead area, don't add them to your own compost at the end of the season—and, of course, don't eat them.

3. Consider gardening in raised beds or containers with clean soil.

4. The Halifax Urban Soil Guide (myweb.dal.ca/ls236198/soilguideonline.pdf) suggests that fruiting plants, like zucchini and tomatoes, take up less lead than root crops or leafy greens. Other fruit varieties with a very low metal uptake are blueberries, apples, and plums.

5. Wash fruits and vegetables grown near busy streets with water and a 1 percent vinegar or 0.5 soap solution; you ingest more lead from eating the dust and dirt on the vegetables than from plant uptake.

6. Highly contaminated soil should be physically removed from your garden.

Arsenic

Arsenic, poisonous to humans, is a natural component of the slate found in Halifax and can contaminate groundwater. Arsenic is also found in pressure-treated lumber; this material should not be used for raised beds where vegetables are grown, and you may also want to rethink planting your edibles right next to a treated wood fence where arsenic leaches out.

Some companies that do soil testing

1. AGAT Laboratories, 11 Morris Drive, Dartmouth (Burnside), NS, or call (403) 299-2000, toll free 1-800-661-7174, (agatlabs.com)
2. MAXXAM Analytics, 200 Bluewater Road, Suite 105, Atlantic Acres Business Park, Bedford, NS, or call (902) 420-0203 or toll free: (800) 565-7227, (maxxam.ca)
3. ALS Labs, 10 Thornhill Drive, Dartmouth, NS, or call (902) 481-0017, (alsglobal.com)

Determining pH levels

Especially if you've had a crop failure in the past, your soil's pH level may be a contributing factor. The pH levels of soil are a measure of its alkalinity or acidity and can be placed along a spectrum in which acid soils have a pH level lower than 7—or pH neutral—and alkaline soils have a pH level higher than 7. Here in the Maritimes, our soils generally tend more towards the acidic—fortunately, a pH level favoured by most vegetables.

Garden centres will sell you a home test kit to give you a general idea of your soil's pH level. For a more accurate reading, you can send a soil sample to a lab that does soil tests, such as the one at the Nova Scotia Agricultural College in Truro.

Once you know the pH level, you can start applying soil amendments to bring the pH level to around neutral—strongly acidic soils can be treated with ground limestone, while very alkaline soils should be treated with sulfur.

Edibles that thrive in slightly alkaline soils (pH 7–8) include asparagus, cabbage, Swiss chard, and broccoli. Edibles that thrive in acidic soils (pH 4.5–5.5) include blueberries, fennel, potatoes, and rhubarb.

To till or not to till

The Rototiller is a marvellous tool that most serious gardeners would find it hard to do without. It churns up hard, compacted earth, chewing up weeds as it goes. In a dozen or so passes, it has turned uninviting sod into a loose growing medium that is reminiscent of coffee grounds, good enough to roll around in.

Much as I hate to admit it, there are drawbacks to tilling. It can break up natural aggregates in the soil and kill off beneficial soil organisms that help plants grow. Tillers are expensive to buy and require regular servicing. Finally, like their power mower cousins, tillers also spew their share of gas fumes into the atmosphere.

There are alternatives to tilling. If you have a small plot and fairly sandy soil, you might consider turning your soil the old-fashioned way: with a shovel. Digging up clumps of soil and loosening them by hand is definitely labour-intensive, but spares a lot of microbiological grief and is easier on the environment—no emissions.

If you really need that tiller (especially if you have heavy clay soil), try to till as little as possible and don't use it as a weeding tool. You can rent a tiller by the day from the garden centre of your nearest Home Depot for around fifty dollars; it's much cheaper than buying one.

A Mantis tiller hard at work

Lasagna Gardening

One way to avoid the tilling debate altogether is to build a layered or "lasagna" garden; this also works well for people with contaminated or otherwise poor soil in their yards. Also known as "sheet composting," the lasagna garden is made up of layers of organic materials piled on top of an existing lawn. The layers slowly break down and become a nutritious and fluffy humus that your plants will love.

There are many benefits to lasagna gardening: it uses materials that you generate in and around your property, such as cardboard, newspapers, kitchen scraps, dead leaves, and grass clippings—no need to visit the garden centre. It also saves you the chore of digging up your lawn.

Once you've chosen a spot for your garden, simply lay down a layer of brown corrugated cardboard or three to four layers of newspaper right on top of your lawn. Wet this first paper layer well with a hose or watering can to keep it in place. The purpose of this first permeable layer is to smother the grass and weeds underneath—earthworms will be able to get through.

A lasagna garden in the making: cardboard underneath, leaves on top

Any material that lands in your green bin or on your compost heap is a suitable candidate for a lasagna garden: grass clippings, leaves, seaweed, manure, pine needles, garden trimmings, peat moss, coffee grounds, fruit and vegetable peelings, egg shells, wood shavings from your pet hamster. As with real lasagna, try to layer your ingredients: alternate a "brown" layer with a "green" one for optimal decomposition (you can refer back to the list of "brown" and "green" compost materials on page 23). Keep piling things on until your garden is about two feet high; this heap will shrink quite dramatically as materials start to break down, but you can keep adding material to create a raised bed.

Autumn is an ideal time to build a lasagna garden because there are so many fallen leaves lying around—if you don't have a deciduous tree on your property, watch for bags of leaves to appear on your neighbourhood garbage night. A lasagna garden built in the fall will also have at least six months to break down and will be kept moist by winter precipitation. If you start your lasagna garden in spring or summer and plan to use it that same season, you should add more "finished" materials to your mix, topping it all off with a few inches of peat moss, well-decomposed compost, or topsoil from a garden centre.

Your "cooked" lasagna garden can be planted just like other gardens—simply dig in! Feed your garden an occasional salad of grass clippings or mowed-over leaves. In the winter, you can throw your kitchen scraps on top and cover with straw, leaves, or dirt, or dig them under, if you're concerned about attracting animals.

And now, let's meet the new summer tenants—vegetables you'll be glad you grew!

CHAPTER 3

Leafy Greens and Legumes

Many of the vegetables in this group, with the exception of beans, can be planted early in the season (mid- to late May in Nova Scotia, usually). This group is truly best eaten fresh—raw or lightly steamed—though the legumes, chard, and spinach can be frozen with success.

Care and Feeding

Leafy plants like lettuce, spinach, and cruciferous veggies—kale, cabbage, broccoli—
need lots of nitrogen (N), which promotes dark green growth (lawn products contain
lots of nitrogen for that reason). Yellowing leaves, especially older leaves, are a sign of
nitrogen deficiency.

Sources of nitrogen include compost or compost tea, alfalfa meal, or blood meal.
Plant legumes like beans and peas nearby; they add nitrogen to the soil that can be
used by other plants.

Leafy Greens

Early Greens

If you are a regular visitor at a farmers' market in Nova Scotia, you'll likely notice the
early salad mixes starting to appear in mid-May. These typically contain a mixture of
early spring greens like arugula, endive, lettuce, beet greens, spinach, pea shoots, and mustard greens.

Growing your own salad is easy, especially in containers, which warm up more quickly than the garden. Start in late April or early May and stay tuned to the weather channel for frost warnings—you

Early arugula, endive, and spinach. Add seed in the gaps left by your first crop and
enjoy an uninterrupted succession of tender, young greens.

can always throw a bedsheet over your patch on a cold night. (Don't forget to take it off the next day.) Use a mixture of garden-centre topsoil and your own compost to add to containers, or just some of your regular garden soil. Make sure the greens get a good dose of compost—spinach is a heavy feeder.

I don't bother with planting these greens in rows; just sprinkle them quite thickly in your patch or container and cover them with a thin layer of soil. Once they've reached a couple of inches in height, you can thin the plants by picking them for your salads, leaving some to go to seed, if you like. (Self-seeded lettuce and spinach are a lazy gardener's delight!)

Because they grow quickly, many greens are good candidates for succession planting—plant a new patch of them every couple of weeks for a fresh supply throughout the season. Keep in mind that many don't like the hot summer sun—reserve shadier spots in your yard for midsummer lettuce. In a full-sun location, plant greens in late summer for a cool fall crop.

Saving seed: lettuce

SUCCESS RATE: Excellent; since lettuce self-pollinates (that is, produces seeds that contain only the plant's own genetic material), lettuce seed will "come true" the next year.

Lettuce will bolt (go to seed) when the weather is hot—watch for a stalk emerging from the centre of the plant and don't eat the leaves at that point, unless you like very bitter lettuce. Keep an eye out for dark seeds to appear on the bolted part of the plant; you can shake the stalk over a paper bag to collect them. Dry indoors for a week before storing in a sealed container.

HISTORY OF LETTUCE

The first known lettuces were weeds growing around the Mediterranean basin some forty-five hundred years ago. This wild lettuce, also known as prickly lettuce (*Lactuca scariola*), appeared in ancient Egyptian tomb paintings, and was used to cure insomnia, to relieve rashes, and to improve fertility. The seeds of the bitter *L. scariola* were also used by the Egyptians to make lettuce oil. Lettuce was brought to the New World by Columbus at the end of the fifteenth century, and was being cultivated in the Bahamas, Haiti, and Brazil by the late sixteenth and early seventeenth centuries.

Saving seed: spinach

SUCCESS RATE: Good, although spinach is wind-pollinated, so if you or your neighbours within 2 kilometres (1 mile) or so are growing different varieties, the strain's purity may be lost. To minimize cross-ups, grow only one variety at a time.

Like lettuce, spinach will start to bolt in hot weather. Watch for yellowing leaves and seed formation along the central stalk. You can pull the plants out and strip off seeds, drying them thoroughly before storing in a sealed container.

A few favourite varieties

(all are open-pollinated; good for seed saving)

LEAF LETTUCE: Bibb, Black-seeded Simpson, Buttercrunch, Red Oak Leaf

SPINACH: Bloomsdale

The early birds: arugula and corn salad (mache)

ARUGULA: For years, I tried to grow this peppery, seductive salad green in midsummer, only to have it chewed up completely by flea beetles. I didn't know then that arugula prefers the cold weather of a Nova Scotia spring, before its predators get going. I've since grown arugula successfully, starting in mid-April (it can be earlier if you're using a cold frame), scatter-shooting it alongside other cold-weather specials like spinach and endive. When it's bolted, I collect the seeds for a late-summer sowing.

CORN SALAD: Also known as "mache," this is another cold weather–loving salad green that thrives in our cool, wet Maritime climate. Master gardener Eliot Coleman awards corn salad high marks as a green that can be eaten well into the winter—and Mr. Coleman lives in Maine, a state with formidable winters. To compensate, he uses cold frames to extend his harvest period. His 1992 book *The New Organic Grower's Four-Season Harvest* explains his technique and makes for inspiring reading. I've listed it in the bibliography.

Beets: a double life

Beets are a versatile veggie: you can pluck a few of their colourful greens to eat steamed with butter or as a salad green early in the season, and then wait for the actual beet to form later in the summer. Some good varieties include Bull's Blood, Detroit Dark Red, and Bassano. The seed of the beet is somewhat larger than lettuce or spinach, but can be sown in a similar closely spaced manner, to be later thinned out and eaten. Watch for those distinctive red or purple stems.

Kale: a lion in winter

Kale is a vegetable that no garden should be without. Along with other cruciferous vegetables like cabbage, broccoli, and Brussels sprouts, the dark-green leafy kale is loaded with glucosinolates, which help the body quickly eliminate carcinogenic substances (it gets high marks in the recently published *Cooking With Foods That Fight Cancer* for that reason).

Red Russian kale—delicious and highly nutritious

Perhaps the best thing about kale is its hardiness: I've carelessly left mine sitting in the garden until December before it showed signs of fatal decline. I probably should have covered it with straw or leaves to have kept it going even longer.

You can start kale from seed along with other early season salad greens; the young, tender leaves of kale are delicious raw. Once it gets bigger, you should thin it out to give several of the largest, healthiest plants room to spread out and mature.

Things to watch out for

Munching insects like flea beetles love kale. I cover it early on in white fabric row cover (see pages 85 and 86). By fall, many of the kale's predators will have died off or gone away, and it will flourish, unchewed and glorious.

A few favourite varieties

(all are open-pollinated; good for seed saving)

CURLY GREEN: This variety has been known to winter over in Nova Scotia.

RED RUSSIAN

SIBERIAN

KALE SALAD

Contents can be altered to suit available produce. In selecting candidates, look for bright colours and crunch.

Cut up six or so good-sized kale leaves into small pieces. Peel and slice two carrots into bite-sized chunks. For extra colour, add a couple of handfuls of chopped red cabbage, or some sliced radish—a few snap peas, if you have them, are an added bonus.

Mix together 1–2 tablespoons (15 to 25 millilitres) of apple cider or balsamic vinegar (lemon juice also works well), 1 tablespoon (15 millilitres) of sesame oil, and a couple of splashes of soy sauce. Toss dressing with salad in a bowl.

Top with chopped parsley, sesame or sunflower seeds, or cashew bits. Let the salad sit for a few minutes before serving to allow flavours to sink in.

Radish

Neither a green nor a legume, radish is included here because it can be planted early and, like greens, it grows quickly and is wonderful in salads. An old favourite variety is Cherry Belle, but many new multicoloured hybrids now exist with names like "Easter Egg mix." Some radishes grow long and carrot-like. Radishes are among the fastest and easiest crops to grow, suitable for children and impatient gardeners. They are lots of fun to pull and a very pretty crop.

Maintenance required/special needs

Sow radish from seed in late April/early May in good, loose soil; it will be ready to pull in just a few short weeks. To maximize garden space, it's a good idea to intersperse fast-growing radish with slower growers like carrots and potatoes; when the radishes are done (they'll taste bitterly sharp and have a woody texture by then), you can pull them out and leave the patch to the late bloomers.

A few favourite varieties

(all are open-pollinated; good for seed saving—but see below)

CHERRY BELLE

FRENCH BREAKFAST (Radishes *are* eaten for breakfast in France—sliced, with bread and butter.)

Saving seed

SUCCESS RATE: Not great for beginners, since radish are pollinated by bees and cross easily with other varieties.

Legumes

Peas

TYPES: edible pods ("snap") and "shell" varieties. Sweet peas have similar foliage to their edible cousins, come in many colours, and smell heavenly.

Maintenance required/special needs

Plant peas from seed in the late spring; they like the cool weather. Pea shoots make a delicious addition to salad, if you're too impatient to wait for the pods.

Plant peas quite close together to maximize space; they don't mind the crowding.

They can be planted in double rows, 4 to 6 inches apart, to make it easier for you if you're building them a trellis. Plant about 4 centimetres (1 ½ inches) deep.

Most peas require some kind of support, though there are some bush varieties that don't need it. Consider planting them next to an existing source of support, like a garage, house, or fence (chain link is excellent). Garden

Sugar snap peas can grow above eight feet and require support.

centres sell plastic mesh netting that can be easily attached to the wooden shingles of your house or shed, or you can use chicken wire or wooden lattice. I watch for discarded hockey sticks and cross-country ski poles on garbage days in the spring—with a little modification, these make good supports for my pea fences.

Veseys Seeds, based in Charlottetown, Prince Edward Island, carries a thirty-dollar expandable steel-wire pea fence that folds up when you're done for the season. It can also be used for cucumbers and pole beans.

Peas and sweet peas are fond of well-composted chicken manure, if you can find it.

A few favourite varieties

(all are open-pollinated; good for seed saving)

ALASKA: A small variety of pea that originated in the 1880s. Quick growers.

CAPUCIJNERS: A Dutch variety with purple pods growing on a 1.2- to 1.8-metre (4- to 6-foot) vine. Pod can be eaten raw when young, or save the dried peas for soup.

SUGAR SNAP: Long, edible pods; sweet and delicious. Nearly 2-metre (6-foot) vines need lots of support.

Saving seed

SUCCESS RATE: Excellent; peas are self-pollinating. Cross-pollination, usually by bees, is unlikely, but just to be sure, plant different varieties of peas at least 3 metres (10 feet) apart.

Peas are easy to collect. Leave a few pods on the vine until they are dry and turn yellowy-brown; you'll be able to hear the peas rattling inside when you shake them. (This stage is usually about a month after the pea harvest.) Leave them in a sunny porch or warm attic to keep drying for a couple of weeks before removing the peas from their pods and storing them in a paper or cloth bag (not a sealed container).

Things to watch out for

Peas can get wormy, especially when they get old. Just discard the wormy ones and eat the rest.

Peas don't like the heat of summer—they seem to do much better in early summer or fall. Planting them in mid-May or mid-August will give them the temperatures they appreciate.

Beans

TYPES: Bush and pole, which require supports. Beans can also be divided into edible pod ("snap") and baking ("shell") beans. The pods of shell beans may be too tough and fibrous to eat. Lovely heirloom varieties used in the Saturday-night baked beans of yesteryear—Jacob's Cattle, Soldier, Yellow Eye—can be found in the Seeds of Diversity directory, or check your local organic food store or your own cupboard. Many of the beans in seed catalogues are the edible pod type.

I remember gazing up as a child at a climbing pole bean , probably a Scarlet Runner, many feet taller than me, amazed by its ambition and virtuosity. The heights to which pole beans aspire—and reach, if given enough support—must have been the inspiration for the Jack and the Beanstalk story.

Purple beans are a colourful variation on the usual green.

Maintenance required/special needs

Plant beans from seed when the soil has warmed; just to be certain, I wait until at least mid-June.

Beans are easy to grow; dig them a furrow a couple of inches deep with your hoe and drop the beans in—they like being close together—then cover them with soil. Be on the lookout for birds that will dig up and eat your bean seeds—mourning doves are big offenders. Because they grow quite quickly, you can succession plant beans at one- to two-week intervals up to eight weeks before the fall frost date for your area; this will give you a steady supply of fresh, new, tender beans throughout summer and into fall.

Green beans climbing a support pole

Putting up supports for pole beans takes a bit of time but saves space in a backyard garden—pole varieties are incredibly prolific and easy to pick (no bending!). If you're growing pole beans, you can make an easy support for them using poles cut from straight tree branches or the trunks of tall, discarded Christmas trees propped into a teepee shape and tied together at the top. Bamboo stakes and even tent poles scrounged on trash night or at a yard sale also make good supports. Veseys carries a commercial "bean tower" for around thirty dollars that will support a number of bean plants at once. Plant beans in a circle and wait for the seedlings to appear before putting up poles. No-shows can be replaced later in the season to maximize space near poles.

Deer love beans: see page 88 for ideas on how to keep them away.

A few favourite varieties
(all are open-pollinated; good for seed saving)

Pole
BLUE LAKE: Elegant shape; fantastic flavour.
KENTUCKY WONDER: These get extremely long and twisty, with a look of arthritic fingers, but have an unbeatable flavour and freeze well. They go on producing well into the fall.
SCARLET RUNNER: Grown as early as 1750, the stunning red blossoms of this variety, which can reach 5.5 metres (18 feet) in height, attract hummingbirds and bees to the garden. The height and vigour of Scarlet Runners also makes them a good choice to plant in front of an unsightly chain link fence or even next to a telephone pole in front of your house. Older Scarlet Runners get tough and fibrous; pick them when they're young for better eating.

Bush
BLACK VALENTINE (SNAP): Beautiful, shiny black seed, also known as "100 from 1" for its productivity.
JACOB'S CATTLE (SHELL AND SNAP): Kidney-shaped red and white spotted bean; makes superb baked beans.
MAINE YELLOW EYE (SHELL): An old favourite in the Maritimes and Maine; excellent in baked beans and soups.

Advantages of home growing

There is a large and flavourful variety of beans out there that you will not be able to find in most stores. Dried beans are a delicious and economical alternative to the canned variety. Beans freeze well, and are fun and easy for kids to grow. Bean plants fix nitrogen in the soil which can then be used by other plants, especially leafy greens, so be sure to plant these two friends close together.

Saving seed

SUCCESS RATE: Excellent; like peas, beans are self-pollinating and only rarely cross-pollinate via the bee.

Saving their large seed is very easy to do. Just leave a few pods hanging on the bush or pole when the plant is dying down in the fall; pods are dry when you can rattle the beans inside. Break open the yellow, brittle pods and harvest the beans for next year's seed or to eat as baked beans or in soups. Store beans in an envelope or paper bag in a cool, dry place.

HISTORY OF BEANS

Beans are one of the longest-cultivated plants in the world, grown and worshipped by the ancient Egyptians, who associated them with immortality. The ancient Greeks, however, believed that beans were evil, caused bad dreams, and even promoted madness. Dour St. Jerome forbade nuns from eating beans, saying they "tickled the genitals."

The pre-Columbian inhabitants of the east coast of North America grew beans, squash, and corn together in an early instance of successful companion gardening: the beans used the corn stalks as a climbing support while providing nitrogen to the other plants; the prickly squash vines kept animal intruders at bay.

Beans played an important role in the history of democracy: in elections and referenda of ancient Greece and Rome, voters dropped a white bean in a jar for "yes" and a black bean in a jar for "no."

Bean-counters

When I was small, my allowance was calculated using a somewhat complicated system of white and black beans, perhaps borrowed from the early Greek democratic process! Each completed daily chore merited a white bean in the large Mason jar in our kitchen while shirking a daily duty (making the bed, drying the dishes, feeding the dog) earned me a black bean. At the end of the week, my mother, the bean-counter, would tally up the legumes: each white bean was worth ten cents, but a black bean could cancel out the value of a white bean.

Whatever leafy greens or legumes you choose to plant, you will soon reap the benefits of their rapid growth and high nutritional value as your garden quickly turns into a well-stocked salad bar. Enjoy!

CHAPTER 4

The Picklers: Tomatoes, Cucumbers, Peppers

Here you'll find those versatile vegetables that are delicious when eaten raw or transformed into sauces, pickles, and relishes for winter storage. These fruiting, warm-weather-loving plants are found in most Maritime gardens.

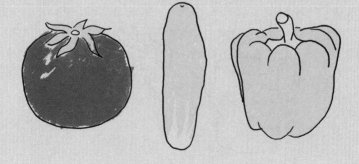

Care and feeding

Fruiting plants like tomatoes, cucumbers, and other squash need lots of phosphorus (P), which is essential for root, flower, and fruit development. The sign of phosphorus deficiency is purple veining in plants. Sources of phosphorus include compost, manure, liquid seaweed, or bone meal.

Tomatoes

TYPES: The classic pincushion shape of the tomato is the standard, but tomatoes come in several shapes, flavours, and sizes—the plum-shaped paste tomato is well-suited to sauces while the miniature cherry tomato is perfect for salads and looks great in a hanging basket.

Maintenance required/special needs

Tomatoes can be started indoors from seed, but should go into the ground as transplants, i.e. when the plants are 10 to 13 centimetres (4 to 5 inches) or taller. Transplants can be found at most garden centres and many farmers' markets from late spring until early summer.

Tomatoes need a full-sun location to flourish: consider putting them in next to a sunny wall or at least a place that is not too windy. If your garden patch is shady, you can put your tomato plant into a container and it will do fine. (Just don't forget to water it—those pots dry out more quickly than a regular garden.)

To heat up your soil for sun-loving tomatoes and peppers, you can put Cozy-Coats (also known as Wall-O-Water) around each plant—these are clear or red plastic sleeves you fill with water from a hose or tap and place around each transplant; the water inside the sleeve gets heated by the sun and, like a small greenhouse, warms the plant inside. Ask for them at your local garden centre.

To plant tomatoes, dig a hole and add some compost or well-rotted manure. Since tomatoes are big consumers of potassium, add some materials that are rich in this mineral: try wood ashes, seaweed, or crushed eggshells. Allow at least 1 foot of space between transplants; you won't believe how big some tomato plants can get. Another way to plant tomatoes is to dig a trench and lay the tomatoes in horizontally, with stems buried up to the lower leaves; this technique will encourage root growth along the stem.

Keep your tomatoes well fertilized with fish emulsion or composted manure tea throughout the growing season; I keep an old watering can handy next to my rain barrel for mixing these strong-smelling amendments in. (You can buy commercial manure teas with names like Barnyard Bounty at most garden centres; they come in a gauze bag that looks remarkably like a regular tea bag. Don't leave them lying around your kitchen if you're an absent-minded tea drinker!)

Most open-pollinated tomato varieties grow large and sprawling: you can give them support with a wire tomato cage or let them lie, placing a bed of eelgrass or straw mulch underneath to keep the fruit from sitting on damp ground and rotting.

Not all tomatoes turn red when ripe: This one, sweet and delicious while still green, is called Green Zebra.

A few favourite varieties

(all are open-pollinated; good for seed saving)

BRANDYWINE: Red, pink, or purple—they're all excellent.

CHERRY: A nice salad addition.

OXHEART: Big, juicy, great flavour.

ROMA: Meaty—great for tomato sauce.

Advantages of home growing

If you're keen on making your own tomato sauce, ketchup, or salsa, plant tomatoes! Tomatoes are very versatile and can be used raw or cooked in many dishes.

If this is your first garden or if you're likely to be away from home for part of the summer, it makes sense to go with a vegetable that can fend for itself a bit; though our family garden has suffered many vicissitudes of weather, insect depredations, and occasional neglect over the years, one vegetable that has always come through has been the tomato. Slugs and deer seem to avoid its foliage, and most plants are prolific producers even in years of extreme dryness or dampness.

These hothouse tomatoes are well over six feet tall.

Until a few years ago, I always bought tomato transplants from a local greenhouse, but lately I've been experimenting with different heirloom varieties from seed I've saved the year before—with great success! Many of these older varieties produce large, bulbous, and oddly shaped fruit, but only if you're comparing them with their middle-of-the-road supermarket cousins. The flavour of the homegrown heirlooms is entirely different from transport-truck-ripened industrial tomatoes and makes you understand why tomatoes are classified as fruit—they are so unbelievably sweet and juicy.

Saving seed: tomatoes

Success rate: Excellent; tomatoes are self-pollinating, although they are occasionally cross-pollinated by insects. It's a good idea to keep different tomato varieties at least 3 metres (10 feet) apart.

Saving seed is very easy to do with tomatoes: simply pick an especially ripe and healthy-looking specimen from your garden, cut it in half and squeeze or scoop the seeds into a glass jar. Allow the pulpy contents to sit at room temperature for several days; this semi-fermentation process helps the seed to build disease resistance. Next, pour the pulp out onto a plate (paper towel and newsprint are not great; the seeds stick to them like glue), separate out as many seeds as you think you'll be able to use or give away next year, and allow them to dry—but not in the sun—for a couple of weeks. When dry, store your tomato seed in an envelope or in a plastic film canister or Ziploc bag in the freezer where it should keep for several years.

HISTORY AND USES OF THE TOMATO

The tomato originated in South America, but was also found further north. It was probably brought back to Europe from Mexico during the first half of the sixteenth century, although, because it is a nightshade—a plant family with some poisonous relatives—many people were afraid to eat tomatoes until late in the nineteenth century. According to Nava Atlas, "the tomato travelled all over Europe under many interesting names. In Italy, it was first called 'pomo dei mori,' [or] apple of the Moors, then 'pomo d'oro,' golden apple. In France and Germany it was considered an aphrodisiac and thus was called, respectively, 'pomme d'amour' and 'liebesapfel,' both meaning apple of love" (*Vegetariana* 126).

Labelling

I grow several varieties of tomatoes and would not be able to tell some of them apart without labelling them. I use Popsicle sticks or coffee stirrers for this purpose, marking in pencil, as rain can blur ink.

A gardening acquaintance of mine uses a pair of metal shears to cut up empty pop cans into long strips and scratches the names of the plants onto the metal with a knife blade.

What to do with green tomatoes

At the end of the growing season, when the risk of frost has sent you scurrying out into the yard to bring in the harvest, you may find yourself with a dishpan full of green, unripe tomatoes. Check them over for signs of blight (dark brown or black spots) and discard the unhealthy-looking ones. If the tomatoes show signs of starting to ripen, stick a few of them in a paper bag with a ripe apple for a week or two and they will finish ripening.

FRESH SALSA

There is nothing like a bowl of salsa made from fresh garden tomatoes and other homegrown veggies and herbs. Here's one that can be easily adapted to suit the ingredients you have on hand:

Chop up 2 medium to large tomatoes into small chunks and dice 1 medium cucumber and/or 1 green, red, or jalapeno pepper. Finely chop a handful of herbs, such as cilantro, basil, or parsley (or a combination of these). Mince 1 or 2 cloves of garlic and 3 or 4 green onions, or a small portion of 1 white onion.

Mix all of the above into a bowl with 2 tablespoons (30 millilitres) of lemon juice or vinegar and a splash or two of olive oil. Add salt and pepper to taste.

Serve with corn chips or as a relish with your dinner.

As for the truly unripe remainders, green tomatoes are a tasty experience, though quite different from their ripe counterparts: tart and almost crispy like a Granny Smith apple. You can fry them up Southern-style, or turn them into chow, a relish that is excellent with fishcakes and burgers. Green tomato mincemeat is a tasty almost-vegetarian alternative to the traditional Christmas pie filling which uses ground beef or venison (see Chapter 8 for tomato recipes).

Cucumbers

TYPES: A common distinction is between pickling and slicing cucumbers: the former tend toward stubby and prickly while the latter are usually slender and smooth-skinned.

Cucumbers can be trained to climb on a trellis, if you're short on crawling space.

Maintenance required/special needs

One way to grow cucumbers is to make a low mound or hill and drop two or three seeds into it (this works well for squash, too). The hills will warm up to temperatures the cukes like. Stir lots of well-composted manure, compost, or other fertilizer into your hills, and allow several metres (feet) between hills. Cucumbers, like their cousins, squash, need room to crawl, although they can be trained to climb on a wooden or metal trellis to save space and for ease of harvesting. This is how they are usually grown in the greenhouse.

A few favourite varieties

NOTE: Many varieties of cucumber today are hybrids; their seed will not "come true" the following year. The following are all open-pollinated varieties.

LEMON

MARKETMORE

STRAIGHT EIGHT

Cucumbers sprawl onto the lawn of the St. Mary's Boat Club in Halifax.

Advantages of home growing

A fresh sliced cucumber sprinkled with salt is one of summer's great delicacies—and what fun to hunt these long green fingers under their prickly, jungle-like canopy!

It's not hard to find bushels of field cucumbers for sale at most farmers' markets and even conventional grocery stores around the end of August. As a pickling fanatic, however, I like to time my activities to suit the size of the cucumbers in the garden: when they're small, it's time to make dill pickles, when they're medium-sized, I pull out the bread and butter pickle recipe, when they're big and ripe, I get ready for ripe cucumber relish. I've included a couple of favourite pickle recipes in Chapter 8.

Saving seed

SUCCESS RATE: Okay if there are no other varieties within about 60 metres (200 feet). Don't try growing more than one cuke variety in your garden or the plants will cross-pollinate. Bees just love the seductive yellow flowers of the cucumber and squash.

If you decide to persevere, leave cukes on the vine until they turn yellow and get fat; this will probably be several weeks after you've finished eating from your patch. Cut the cucumber in half lengthwise and scoop out the seed and pulp into a bowl of water; leave this at room temperature for a few days to allow the mixture to ferment and stir often to keep mold from forming. The good seeds are heavy and will sink to the bottom of the bowl; pick these out and dry them on a plate or other non-paper surface for a couple of weeks, and then store in a cool, dry place.

Things to watch out for

The striped cucumber beetle once ravaged my entire crop (though it left the other members of the squash family alone) by chewing the tiny cuke sprouts off at the base and devouring their leaves.

These small, yellow and black striped terrors—unlike the slow-moving potato beetle—are almost impossible to catch and squish with your bare hands since they fly away at the slightest threat. I dosed my plants with wood ash against the onslaught, but the damage was already done. I didn't plant any cucumbers the next year, hoping that the beetles would not overwinter in my garden. Perhaps it was sheer luck, but I haven't seen a beetle in the fifteen years since.

Peppers

Types: Both sweet and hot varieties can be grown in Nova Scotia, though I've had more success with the hot ones: they are generally smaller and seem to mature more quickly.

A sweet yellow pepper hides beneath its leafy canopy.

Maintenance required/special needs

Peppers are heat-loving plants; they don't flourish in Mexico for nothing! Make sure to plant them in a sunny location. Peppers get big, so provide them with some support when they start to produce fruit—tomato cages work well. Too much nitrogen in the soil will produce a lushly-leafed pepper plant with few fruit, so go easy on the fertilizer.

Peppers make good container candidates; the generally drier soil conditions in a pot suit the hot varieties perfectly. I've heard of gardeners who bring their potted pepper plants inside for the winter where they lie dormant before coming back to life the next spring.

A few favourite varieties

(all are open-pollinated—many peppers sold in garden centres and the ones you buy at the grocery store are hybridized and so won't produce the same fruit as the parent plant)

SWEET: Lipstick, Sweet Banana, Sweet Chocolate
HOT: Early Jalapeno, Habanero, Hungarian Yellow Wax Hot

Things to watch out for

Cutworms may try to attack your peppers at the base of their stem. Protect seedlings by putting a cardboard or plastic collar around the base of the plant. Cut-up milk cartons and yogourt containers work well for this purpose.

Saving seed

SUCCESS RATE: Very good; peppers are self-pollinating, though bees may cause different varieties of neighbouring peppers to cross-pollinate.

Allow the pepper to ripen beyond the eating stage; it will turn from green to red (or, depending on the variety, yellow, orange, or purple) and will start to shrivel. Because peppers take a long time to ripen and our summers are short, you can bring nearly ripe ones indoors to finish ripening in a warm window.

Cut open your pepper and remove the seeds; allow them to dry for at least two weeks before storing.

Most of the vegetables we've considered thus far, whether destined for the salad bowl, the steamer, or the sandwich, are delicious but short-lived, rather like summer itself. In the following chapter, let me introduce you to some veggies that you can keep around for a much longer time.

CHAPTER 5

Good Keepers: Root Crops and Squash

These vegetables share the distinction of being good winter keepers; they won't require refrigeration and will keep for several months in a cool place. Many vegetables in this group—potatoes, carrots, beets, turnips, onions, and garlic—grow their fruit underground, while others, like winter squash, grow their fruit in the shade of their enormous leaves.

Care and feeding

Root crops such as carrots, potatoes, and garlic take lots of potassium (K), which promotes frost resistance and helps them to resist disease. Stunted leaves, splotches of yellow on older leaves, or scorched-looking leaves are all signs of potassium deficiency. Sources of potassium include compost, kelp meal, and composted wood ash (for acidic soils).

Potatoes

TYPES: Plain, starchy, and comforting, potatoes come in red-, white-, and blue-skinned varieties, as well as yellow-fleshed. An unusual variation is the "All Blue" variety, whose blue flesh makes a colourful companion with white fish or chicken on the dinner plate.

A bushel of newly harvested Chieftain potatoes

Maintenance required/special needs

Planting potatoes is a bit different from sowing other kinds of seed. For one thing, you're using the actual vegetable as seed, so you'll need a shovel (rather than a hoe) to dig down deep enough to plant it.

To prepare for planting, cut your seed potato into two or three pieces, making sure each piece has an "eye" (or sprout) on it. Allow the pieces to "heal over" for a couple of hours before planting. Dig a hole several inches deep for each seed piece, stick it in, sprout side up, cover and mound each hill up slightly with soil or mulch to protect the tubers from sunlight. If they're not well covered, potatoes will turn green and poisonous.

I've heard of putting the head or tail of a mackerel or other fish part in with the seed to give the potato an extra boost of nutrition as it grows.

> "Human nature will not flourish, any more than a potato, if it be planted and replanted, for too long a series of generations, in the same worn out soil."
>
> Nathaniel Hawthorne, *The Scarlet Letter*

UNCLE MEDFORD'S TATTIE DROTTLE (POTATO SOUP)

One of my childhood favourites, this easy and wonderfully comforting soup will warm you up on a cold day.

5 cups (1.2 litres) of potatoes, sliced thinly
1 medium onion
¼ cup (50 millilitres) chopped celery
1 cup (250 millilitres) water
1 teaspoon (5 millilitres) salt
3 tablespoons (45 millilitres) butter
2½ cups (625 millilitres) milk
1 tablespoon (15 millilitres) chopped parsley

Cook potatoes, onion, and celery in water and salt in a heavy pot until vegetables are tender. Mash everything together, add butter, milk, and parsley. Heat through (don't let it boil) and serve.

Things to watch out for

Many potato growers wage an annual battle with the Colorado potato beetle, a medium-sized striped yellow and black insect that can chew the leaves of the potato down to stubs. See Chapter 7 for some help with this pest that seems to be able to seek out your potato plants even in areas where potatoes don't normally grow (i.e., your urban backyard!).

A wet summer can really do damage to growing potatoes: imagine spending most of your life sitting in mud. Wet potatoes are susceptible to rot (the smell is unmistakable), and there's really nothing you can do about it. Three weeks of non-stop rain one August destroyed two-thirds of our potato crop.

The potato harvest is an annual late-summer joy.

HISTORY OF THE POTATO

Like its cousin the tomato, the potato was first cultivated six thousand to seven thousand years ago by the natives of Peru, where the hardy vegetable grew well in the high altitudes of the Andes mountains. Prized for its good storage qualities and nutritional value, the potato was brought back to Europe by the Spanish conquistadors, and finally made its way to North America with the English settlers of the sixteenth century. The Great Potato Famine of 1845–49 in Ireland brought millions of starving refugees to North America.

In more recent history, in 1995 the potato became the first vegetable to be grown in space. Currently, one-third of the world's potatoes are grown by India and China, countries better known for their rice than their spuds.

A few favourite varieties

These varieties are often grown in the Maritimes. You will see these at some farmers' markets.

CHIEFTAIN: Red skin and white flesh—a good producer. Keeps well in a cool cellar.

KENNEBEC: Good mid-season variety with white flesh.

FINGERLING: A German variety, just a bit thicker than a cigar; it has a slightly stronger flavour than most potatoes, and a moist texture.

IRISH COBBLER: The classic old-fashioned potato: humble and lumpy. Flesh is dry and tasty.

YUKON GOLD: A beautiful yellow-fleshed variety that does well in our Maritime climate. Lots of lovely potatoes in each hill.

Advantages of home growing

Who doesn't like potatoes? Mashed, baked, boiled, or fried, they are an unparalleled comfort food. Digging potatoes when the plants have died back in early fall is great fun for kids, whose keen eyes and nimble fingers are great harvesting aids.

Saving seed

SUCCESS RATE: Very good, as long as the potato hasn't rotted; give your spuds a sniff now and then to make sure they're still sound. Over the winter, the "eyes" (or seed sprouts) of untreated potatoes will grow into long, pale, twisty arms as they reach for the light; the energy required to do this will wither the poor tuber. Snip these off as soon as you notice them (the earlier, the better) and reserve those taters for next year's seed, as our forebears once did. Keep them in a paper bag, or a wooden or wicker basket in a cool, dark place.

Carrots

TYPES: The traditional bright orange carrot has been joined by different-coloured varieties: yellow, white, and blue. A round, radish-like variation on the traditional pointer-finger shape of the carrot makes growing this root crop possible even for container gardeners.

Maintenance required/special needs

Carrots have quite small, fine seed and take a long time to germinate, so long, in fact, that you may forget they're there. Because of this slow germination process, weeds will try to take over the carrot patch—try to stay on top of them while your carrots establish their roots. Carrots like loose, well-aerated soil; add some bone meal when you're preparing the bed to help with root development.

Carrots grow slowly, but are worth waiting for.

HISTORY OF CARROTS

The wild carrot was indigenous to Europe and parts of Asia, growing there as early as ten thousand years ago. The seeds of the wild carrot were used medicinally. The name *carota* for the cultivated carrot was first found in the writings of the Roman Athenaeus around 200 AD.

When the carrot tops are a couple of inches tall, it's time to thin them; this step is necessary to give the remaining carrots space to grow bigger. (It's very hard to sow carrot seed thinly enough to not have to pull some of them out as babies.) Pull out carrots that seem closely bunched together. To avoid pulling the whole clump out, you can use scissors to snip away the tops of the smaller carrots, leaving the biggest one to grow.

You can leave carrots in the soil even after the first fall frost, which, while it may knock down the carrot tops, won't affect the root.

If you find the tops keep breaking off the carrots when you're trying to pull them out, try using a shovel to dig them out instead.

A few favourite heirloom carrot varieties

CHANTENAY RED CORED: 1830s French variety; about 5 inches long, tender and sweet

DANVERS: Developed around 1947 in Springfield, Massachusetts, this is a good heat-tolerant variety.

THUMBELINA: Round like a radish—good for container gardens

TOUCHON

Advantages of home growing

A freshly pulled carrot has a flavour all its own; most people, and many pets, really enjoy them raw.

Carrots are wonderful winter keepers: store them in a box, basket, or cooler full of sawdust (make sure the sawdust came from untreated lumber!) in your basement or other cool place.

Saving seed

SUCCESS RATE: Not great. Carrots are biennials, meaning you won't be able to harvest their seed until the second year. They are insect-pollinated, and frequently cross with other members of the carrot family, including Queen Anne's Lace, a common roadside weed. Many varieties of carrot are hybrids.

Squash

NOTE: I have included information on growing summer squash—not good keepers—alongside their winter brethren since growing requirements are similar for both.

TYPES: Summer squash, like zucchini, will need to be kept in the fridge. Winter varieties (including pumpkins) will keep for several months in a cool, dry place.

Maintenance required/special needs

Squash are very easy to grow, but require space to crawl. Don't plant more than a few in the city unless you are prepared to give up a chunk of your lawn. Squash are heavy feeders, liking lots of compost or manure mixed with their soil. Hill up a dinner plate–sized mound and drop two or three seeds around the perimeter. Allow lots of space between hills.

Keep a regular feeding schedule once blossoms have formed and fruit is setting and growing. I add compost or manure as a "side dressing," or use a liquid fish fertilizer—not great in the city if you have cats that are attracted to the smell.

Squash are good keepers, but the damp coolness of a root cellar may speed up spoilage. An unheated attic or other dry, cool room in the house would be a better bet.

Some of the squash varieties in this wheelbarrow include acorn, Hubbard, buttercup, and pumpkin.

A few favourite heirloom varieties

Winter squash

BURGESS BUTTERCUP: A good old Maritime variety, this one looks like a flattened turban.

DELICATA: A small, yellow and green striped variety with incredibly sweet flavour.

HUBBARD: Known for its bulk—a Hubbard squash can tip the scales at 4–7 kilograms (10–15 pounds)—and its warted skin, this is a truly delectable squash with a dry texture and nutty flavour. Comes in golden, blue, and dark-green varieties.

TABLE QUEEN ACORN: Lovely, smooth dark-green skin; wonderful baked. Its bowl shape lends itself to stuffing.

WALTHAM: Beige skin, long neck, and bulbous bottom, yet another delectable squash. It's great roasted, baked, on its own, or in soups.

Summer squash

PATTAPAN: Attractive, light-green, flying saucer–shaped squash with crenellated edges: serve like yellow crooknecks.

VEGETABLE SPAGHETTI: A wonderful alternative to pasta, especially for the gluten intolerant, the long, stringy yellow fibres live up to the name and can be enjoyed with tomato sauce or pesto.

YELLOW CROOKNECK: Sliced and steamed, this zucchini-like squash is superb served with garlic butter.

Advantages of home growing

I consider members of the squash family to be among the most impressive of all vegetables for the sheer size they attain in a relatively short period of time, and with little to no human encouragement. The shade beneath their giant, prickly, tropical-looking leaves provides a sheltered nursery for the numerous fruit that can grow to an overwhelming size—just ask the friends who snuck that baseball bat–sized zucchini into the back seat of your car last summer!

The zucchini is nearly as big as Penny!

DESPERATION SOUP FOR THE ZUCCHINI INVASION

Summer squash like zucchini and yellow crookneck can really take off in mid-August, leaving you scrambling for ways to use them up. I invented this soup recipe the year the zucchini threatened to flatten the house.

To make Desperation Soup, peel and slice two potatoes and one medium onion. Cover them with water and boil them in a pot until potatoes are tender. If you have a vegetable or chicken bouillon cube on your shelf, add it too; if not, add a few shakes of salt to taste. Meanwhile, slice up one medium-sized zucchini, pattypan, yellow crookneck, or other summer squash and add to the nearly done potato/onion.

Transfer the contents of the pot to a blender or food processor, along with a handful of fresh parsley, basil, and chives (or any other herbs you have growing nearby).

Grate about a half-cup (125 millilitres) of hard cheese—Cheddar, Gouda, or Parmesan are good choices—into the blender and purée the soup. Serve immediately with a dollop of butter on top.

HISTORY OF SQUASH

Early inhabitants of North America grouped squash, corn, and pole beans together in their gardens. Beans fix nitrogen in the soil for their companion plants, while making use of the tall cornstalks nearby to climb on. The extensive prickly stems and vines of the squash, spreading out horizontally rather than vertically, served to deter marauders like raccoons, completing the "three sisters'" symbiotic relationship.

Saving seed

SUCCESS RATE: Good, though with a caveat. Squash are classified into four species with the Latin names *Cucurbita pepo* (includes all acorn squash, all crookneck and zucchini varieties, and most pumpkins), *Cucurbita maxima* (the turban, Hubbard, and buttercup squashes), *Cucurbita moschata* (the butternut and cheese varieties), and *Cucurbita mixta* (silver-seeded gourds). You are safe from cross-breeding if you plant only one of each of the four species each year; two of the same species, planted within 800 metres of each other, will produce some strange-looking squash next year. There are ways to avoid cross-ups, like bagging the squash blossoms and pollinating them by hand rather than relying on the wind or insects, but this is quite a lot of work, especially if you're a beginner.

To harvest the seed, cut open the squash when it is ripe, scoop out the seed, and let dry on newspaper or a plate for a couple of weeks before storing.

Halloween squash

In recent years, pumpkin u-picks have begun to spring up around the province just before Halloween for those who'd rather not devote the back-yard space to growing their own jack o' lantern. In years when my pumpkins failed but other squash flourished, I've carved some unusual-looking grinners on October 31 out of crenellated pattypans and elongated yellow crooknecks that have passed their best. (If the story is to be believed, some of the first jack o' lanterns were made of turnips, not pumpkins, anyway.)

How to cut a squash (the lazy way)

Cutting through the thick skins of pumpkins and squash in order to prepare them for cooking can be a challenging, even dangerous, proposition. The knife slips easily off the rounded, solid flesh and it's easy to get cut.

If your squash is small enough (Acorn, Waltham, Delicata) you can bake it whole in the oven and cut it open and scoop out the seeds when it's cooked.

If you're dealing with a larger variety, like Hubbard, you may need to take drastic measures. I've heard of people actually hitting squash with an axe, but I think I've discovered a safer, if perhaps messier, method. Put your squash in a plastic grocery bag and tie the end; now wrap it in a second bag and tie that one.

If you live in a house with a cement floor in the basement, stand at the top of the steps and throw the squash down onto the floor. (Make sure no one is coming up the stairs first!) It should smash into manageable chunks that you can now bake or boil. If you don't have a cement surface in your house (patio stones in the yard would be a good substitute), you can hurl your squash onto the sidewalk out front, preferably from a height. Neighbours will think you've gone crazy; ignore them! (Or invite them over for a piece of squash pie later…) A great all-around anger management technique.

Onions

TYPES: From the green shallot ("bunching") to the Spanish and other globe onions, the pungent allium is a versatile veggie that can be eaten raw or cooked. Perennial onion will come back every spring and is a good choice for its tasty green shoots.

Maintenance required/special needs

> Onion's skin, very thin,
> Mild winter's coming in.
> Onion's skin, thick and tough,
> Coming winter's cold and rough.
>
> —Old proverb

Onions are usually bought as "sets"—basically, baby onions that were started the year before. (Onions are biennial; that is, their reproductive cycle, or seed-making phase, takes place during the second year.) You can sow your own onion seed, then dig up the little onions and store them over the winter for next year's sets, but this takes a bit of advance planning.

Onions like a long growing season, so start them as soon as you can get into the garden in the late spring.

Because of their shallow roots, onions have a hard time competing with weeds for water, so it's important to start them

A late-summer onion patch

in a weed-free area and to keep up with weeding throughout the season. Not doing this will mean you end up with very small onions. I have used black fabric cloth or landscaping paper over my onion patch to help with weed control—just don't forget to poke holes in the sheeting for each onion; allow 7–10 centimetres (3–4 inches) between holes.

Onions are fairly good winter keepers if they are properly cured: pull them when the green tops have died down in the early fall. (This is a fun job! If the tops break off in your hand, try digging up the onions with a shovel.) Allow them to dry indoors for about a week; a sun porch or other dry area works really well. I lay mine across the top of a wooden clothes drying rack. Store them in net bags (you can save these from the onions you bought in the winter) and keep them away from moisture which will encourage the onions to sprout and will reduce their storage life.

MEDICINAL ALLIUM

Onions and garlic have antiseptic, even antiviral properties, so eat lots in the cold and flu season. If their pungent odour bothers you, you can buy deodorized garlic capsules at drug and health-food stores.

Saving seed

SUCCESS RATE: Not great for beginners; most onions take two years to go to seed, so onion sets are a better bet.

A wooden clothes rack can double as an onion and garlic dryer.

Garlic

I discovered only recently that garlic grows beautifully in Nova Scotia—the Chinese and Filipino provenance of most grocery-store garlic had me wrongly convinced it must be an exotic. It is shockingly easy to grow.

TYPES: Some catalogues divide garlic into "hardneck" and "softneck" varieties; this distinction is important only if you like to braid your garlic and hang it up as an edible decoration (hanging garlics up in a bunch or braid is a space-saving method of curing them). Here are some good varieties, found in the Seeds of Diversity exchange directory:

GERMAN PORCELAIN: Medium-large variety with beautiful white skin.

OTIS TOMAS: A hardy Cape Breton rocambole variety named for the man who's grown it for the past thirty-five years.

ROCAMBOLE: Also known as Spanish garlic or serpent garlic, the cloves of the rocambole have pretty pink skin with purple streaking.

These spring garlics were planted the previous fall.

Maintenance required/ special needs

Much like the spring flower bulbs we plant in the fall, individual garlic cloves can be planted around Thanksgiving for harvest the following July or August. This requirement means a bit of advance planning on the gardener's part.

I make my garlics a nice rich bed of manure or compost in a corner of the garden and cover them with old straw or eelgrass against the winter chill. Each clove will form its own whole bulb, putting up delightful long green shoots in the spring along with the daffodils and tulips.

Be sure to snap off the long, curvy goosenecks (also called scapes) of the garlic plant, prominent in late June and early July, which take the plant's energy away from the bulb. These goosenecks have a mild garlic flavour and are delicious chopped up in a salad or soup.

When the leaves have died down and the stem turns yellow, usually later in August, your garlic is ready to be harvested. Use a shovel to dig up the bulbs, which will be quite firmly entrenched in the soil. I lay my garlics out to dry alongside the onions on my wooden clothes rack in the sun porch. You can do this outside if you have a week of sunny weather in the forecast. Garlics will keep well over the winter and you can use their bulbs as seed; most store-bought garlic can also be used as seed.

Now that you've got your winter's supply of root crops and squash safely stowed away in your basement, it's time to turn our attention to some easy-growing plants that will spice up your winter menu.

CHAPTER 6

About Herbs (and Some Native Perennial Favourites)

Herbs are truly a subject unto themselves; their aesthetic, culinary, and medicinal properties have been celebrated throughout the centuries and in a vast accumulation of literature. I will touch on only a few favourites that work well in Nova Scotia's climate and cuisine.

TYPES: Perennial and annual herbs. Not all herbs are created equal: perennials—plants that can live for several years without needing to be replanted—such as mint, chives, lovage, and sorrel, will come back year after year no matter what neglect they've suffered at your hands. Annuals are less hardy plants that die off after just one growing season; annual herbs like basil, cilantro (also known as coriander), dill, and summer savory will need to be planted every year.

Set aside a special, permanent bed for the perennials, or a special corner of your garden, or even a few dedicated containers. Keep in mind that many perennial herbs originated in a hot, Mediterranean climate and should not be watered often but allowed to dry out—pick a sunny spot for your lavender and rosemary plants and leave them be.

In warm winters, some of your herbs (and other vegetables and annual flowers) may seed themselves. I was thrilled and surprised one spring to discover a haphazard patch of cilantro and Bibb lettuce growing in the garden in early June alongside some young sunflowers already turning their heads to face the sun.

A few favourite varieties

Basil: the saucy herb

Basil is a must for those who enjoy Italian cuisine. It is superb in tomato sauces, and it actually grows companionably next to tomatoes in the garden, supposedly improving their flavour. Pesto is the main reason I grow so much basil: the concentrated flavours of fresh basil, garlic, and parsley are sublime.

You can clone a basil plant by breaking off the flowering tip of the plant and sticking it directly into a fresh pot of soil.

Chives are a perennial standby.

Cilantro leaves are a must for Thai cuisine.

Comfrey grows very quickly.

Chives: the onion stand-in

This hardy perennial grows well in both garden beds and containers. Chives grow in a tall bunch, topped by round, purplish flower heads where the seeds grow—keep an eye on these as the seeds ripen and turn black. You won't need to save seed unless you want to grow a pot of chives in your window during the winter. They are delicious in soups, salads, and dips.

Cilantro: the international herb

Cilantro (the leaves of the coriander plant) features prominently in many national cuisines, from the salsas of Mexico, to the Pad Thais of Thailand, to the curries of India. This refreshing herb with a clean, astringent taste is easy to grow and the seeds of the coriander plant can be kept and used in cooking, although Nava Atlas, author of *Vegetariana,* reminds us that the leaves and seeds of the coriander have two entirely different flavours and cannot be used interchangeably.

Comfrey: a gardener's comfort

If you like your herbs to do more than simply provide a garnish for your dinner, may I suggest the amazing comfrey? This hardy perennial may be snipped off when its leaves are small in the spring to add to your salad (they have a slightly woolly texture). Its tiny, purple bell-shaped flowers are also favourites of bees—and you want lots of those to help with pollination in your garden.

Comfrey leaves make great compost, so go ahead and hack your comfrey back when it gets unwieldy—it will grow back really fast—and throw the leaves on that pile; or soak them in a bucket of water for several weeks to make a potassium-rich liquid plant food that is a hit especially with tomatoes.

If all of that weren't enough to get you planting comfrey, it's good to have around if you happen to fracture a bone: comfrey's other names are "knit bone" and "bone set." According to Earth Clinic: folk remedies and holistic cures (earthclinic.com), comfrey contains allantoin, "which promotes the growth of connective tissue, bone, and cartilage." This website recommends simmering fresh comfrey leaves to make a sticky paste for external application; like arnica, it's good for cuts and bruises, too.

Dill: the pickling herb

I am a huge fan of dill pickles and grow this aromatic herb every year along with cucumbers to feed my addiction. The dill will get to be about half a metre (two or so feet) high and will grow a cylindrical seed crown, which is the part you'll want to use for pickling. (The seed itself makes a good seasoning in soups.)

Dill is an indispensable addition to pickles and soups.

Mint: delicious but invasive!

This is a versatile herb to have around—it's wonderful in salads and as a garnish; you can even make your own mint sauce for roast lamb or steep the leaves in hot water for a refreshing mint tea. Be warned, though, that mint is an invasive plant and can really take over your garden: it's wise to confine it to a container or an area away from the rest of your garden where it can spread harmlessly.

Mint is wonderful as a garnish or in tea.

Parsley can be kept on a sunny windowsill for winter use.

Chances are, you know some folks who already have mint living in their yard: ask them if you can come and dig some up for your container rather than going out and buying it at a garden centre—this is a bit like buying a weed!

Parsley: the slow-growing biennial herb

Parsley is one of the most common and useful of culinary herbs; it is also one of the slower growing seeds. It's a good idea to soak your parsley seed in warm water for a couple of days just before you plant it—this will dissolve the growth inhibiter that covers the parsley seed coat.

To maximize space, plant parsley among quicker growing vegetable varieties like radish and arugula; when they are finished, you can pull them out and allow the parsley its day in the sun.

Summer savory: the stuffing herb

There is nothing like dried summer savory as a poultry seasoning. It will grow into a little, leafy shrub which can be pulled out in the fall and hung upside down in bunches to dry in a warm attic or other room.

The aromatic leaves of summer savory go well in stuffing

Companionable Herbs

Many herbs make good companions for vegetables and flowers—here are a few
examples of plants that grow well together:

HERB	VEGETABLE/FLOWER	BENEFIT TO VEGETABLE
Garlic	Rose	Repels aphids
Basil/oregano	Tomato	Improves taste
Hyssop/onion	Cabbage	Repels cabbage moths
Lovage	All vegetables	General health

A tip for drying herbs

Find a screen from an old window in your house, or on the street awaiting garbage pick
up (it doesn't matter if the screen has a few small holes). Make sure to clean and rinse
it well. Place it in a warm place with no breeze—a stuffy attic is good, or a sunny porch.
You can prop your screen between two chairs or on a couple of stacked phone books
or bricks. Make sure your herbs are clean and free of dirt. Arrange them on the screen,
trying not to overlap too much. My two favourite drying herbs are basil and summer
savory because they keep their flavour so well, but you can try others: dill, cilantro,
parsley, rosemary, oregano, thyme, and mint.

Native plants

If you decide to establish a permanent bed for your perennial herbs, why not consider offering a home to some native Nova Scotian edible plant species at the same time? The advantages of growing natives in your backyard are numerous. They are better suited to the climate (thus requiring less care), you will be encouraging biodiversity by adding these plants, and you may also reduce the diseases brought by imported plants.

Gooseberries grow well in Nova Scotia and make a deliciously tart jam or jelly.

Here are a few native plants that will produce delicious results throughout the summer months (these are all perennials):

blackberry

blueberry

chokecherry (a great choice for jelly-making)

currant

elderberry (often made into wine)

gooseberry

high-bush cranberry (these are very sour, but can be made into jelly)

raspberry

If you're planning on staying in the same house for a few decades, why not plant a couple of sugar maples in the yard? Sugar maples are a native species, too, and I'm certain you're familiar with the deliciousness of their sap when it is boiled into syrup.

For a first-hand account of the benefits of hosting native species on your property instead of the usual expanse of grass, you can take a short online video tour of Halifax professor Bill Freedman's south end Halifax yard, made up entirely of native species (ecologyaction.ca/content/healthy-lawns).

It seems a shame that many urban native-plant enthusiasts are the victims of unsightly premises complaints from neighbours when, from a biodiversity standpoint, such unconventional-looking properties are doing far more good than harm, especially in an urban ecosystem.

Whether or not you decide to turn your lawn into an herbal garden of Eden or a native plant paradise, I wish you the best of success—and no visits from a bylaw enforcement officer!

CHAPTER 7

Uninvited Garden Flora and Fauna

There's no getting around it: at some point in the season, every gardener has to contend with critters eager to wreak havoc on the veggies, with results ranging from the merely irritating to the truly devastating. That patch of weeds that looked so small and inoffensive last week when you decided to go to the beach is, this week, threatening world domination. Keep this section bookmarked for when uninvited guests pay you a surprise visit.

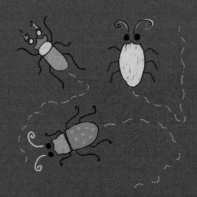

Why natural insect control?

Halifax has a somewhat lopsided pesticide bylaw, which, while allowing retailers to sell chemical lawn and garden pesticides, places the onus on the consumer not to use them. Garden centres in Halifax are required to post information on the bylaw along with information on less harmful alternatives. (It should be noted that, as of the time of this writing, several Canadian provinces including Ontario and Quebec have passed more sweeping cosmetic pesticide bylaws, banning the sale and use of pesticides province-wide. Hopefully, Nova Scotia will soon join this list.)

Many of the pesticides the bylaw covers include chemicals that have been proven to cause cancer and other serious illnesses; their effects can be particularly harmful to growing children whose cells are multiplying quickly. Don't use them!

Vigilance is key to a successful counterattack on insect depredations in the garden: some pests are large and sluggish enough to be picked off plants by hand, while others, particularly those ones with wings and a persistent attitude, will necessitate more drastic measures.

Some tools that belong in every organic gardener's arsenal

1. Floating row cover

The best way to discourage insects from feasting on your plants is to deny them access; this is especially true for flying pests like cabbage moths and striped cucumber beetles. Lee Valley carries rolls of translucent white fabric row cover (see photo next page) that allows sunshine and rain through to the growing seedling while foiling insect intruders. Once your seedling pokes its head through the ground (or even a bit before that happens), you simply unfurl the covering over its head, making sure the cover is well staked to the ground. (I pile quantities of earth along its length so nothing crawls in underneath.) Because the plant will have to live most of its life under this white tent, make sure you don't stretch the cover taut against the seedling; this will stunt its growth.

Plants that have benefited from row covering in my garden over the years include arugula, bok choy, cabbage, and broccoli.

White row cover and flapping tinsel from a used car lot protect this garden from insects and deer.

2. Bt (*Bacillus thuringiensis*)

This is a natural bacterium that proves lethal once in the digestive tracts of caterpillars and beetles, though it is considered safe for humans. I've had to use it on my cabbages and broccoli when I didn't get the row cover down in time. Bt can be sprayed or dusted directly onto your plants; the insects will die after ingesting it. Check your garden supply store for this product.

3. A can of soapy water or salt and a pair of gloves

Hand-picking is the tried and true method for getting rid of potato beetles and slugs—drown them and add the corpses to your compost heap (be sure they're really dead first). Salt desiccates and kills the slimy slug.

Know the enemy: profiles of the opposition

Cats

Outdoor cats can be the bane of the city gardener's existence; they are very fond of using a garden patch as a litter box and like to dig holes in the bare earth, often uprooting tender seedlings.

If you have a dog who likes to spend time in the backyard during the growing season, you have an advantage, although many feline visits occur at night after your guard is off-duty and asleep in the house.

I've tried many of the usually recommended cat repellents (homemade and commercial cayenne-based sprays and pellets, eucalyptus oil, orange peels, plastic netting) with very little success. I did find covering bare patches of earth with a heavy mulch (hay, straw, or eelgrass) reduced the number of smelly cat feces I had to pick up in the morning. Mulching also helps keep weeds down and keeps the earth underneath moist, reducing the need for watering.

I've also heard that coffee grounds are unappealing to felines: a good thing, since the grounds contain valuable nitrogen that the garden can use anyway—if you're even a moderate caffeine addict, you'd be surprised how much of the stuff you'll generate! Another obvious source of grounds is your local coffee shop: ask if they mind giving you some.

Colorado Potato Beetle

This bug has an amazing ability to locate and devour the leaves of potato plants, leaving you with bare, chewed stems. The best treatment, as mentioned before, is hand-picking and drowning the beetles in soapy water. Check the undersides of leaves for their orange-coloured eggs and scrape those off too.

A juvenile Colorado potato beetle in action

Cutworms

These beasties launch a covert attack on plants just beneath the surface of the soil, severing the plant from its root. An effective deterrent against this damaging insect is to make "collars" for your plants (most young plants are susceptible to cutworm attacks) out of milk cartons with their bottoms cut out, or cans with top and bottom removed. Push the collar several centimetres (inches) into the soil around your plant (preferably

while it is still small) to form a barrier against cutworm intrusion.

Do not confuse cutworms with earthworms! Earthworms tunnel through your garden and help aerate the soil; they munch through compost and their castings (droppings) add nutrients to the soil. Many bird species—such as robins, bluejays, and sparrows—find cutworms a delicacy.

Cutworms cut short the lives of baby seedlings.

Deer

Almost every country gardener I've ever talked to has a deer story; these large vegetarians like nothing better than to munch their way through your garden as though it were a specially planted salad bar.

Acquaintances outside Lunenburg have said that their deer visitors are quite capable of clearing the 2-metre (8-foot) chicken-wire fence they put up to discourage them. Another friend has told me that she's found meat meal works well to repel them, though I've never been able to find it at a garden store (and if it's anything like blood meal, meat meal will attract dogs).

I have found that a noisy garden is a safe garden: five years ago, I called all the used-car lots in my area to see if any of them would sell me some of the colourful, metallic banner they use to decorate their lots. One of them gave me about 30 metres (100 feet) of the stuff attached to a nylon rope, and I have used it ever since. There is no doubt that my garden looks tacky with its perimeter of now-bedraggled plasticized foil, but I've had no return visits from the deer that once gorged on my pole beans and carrot tops. I've supplemented the flapping foil with recycled aluminum pie plates tied to wooden posts with twine for added noisiness. (See page 86 for a photograph.)

Fortunately, our property gets its share of breeze to keep the distracting sounds fairly continuous.

At the Spryfield Urban Farm Museum Society, which is often visited by deer, the beds are fenced in and ingeniously topped with long strips of surveyors' tape radiating from a central post, like the ribs of an open umbrella. The deer associate the tape with a roof, and, not liking to feel enclosed, leave the garden alone.

Here are some other suggestions for deer repelling—although I have not tried all of these, so cannot attest to their success. Sprinkled soap shavings (the stronger the fragrance, the better: try Irish Spring); baby powder, sprinkled on plant leaves (or dryer sheets); human hair (spread around or hung in a cloth bag near your veggies—ask your barber or hairdresser for a bagful); chili powder, cayenne pepper, or fresh hot pepper

An anti-deer device at the Spryfield Urban Farm Museum garden (see page 120)

(add to water in your blender, let sit overnight, then strain through a cheesecloth and add to a spray bottle). Bob Matthews, who runs a home gardening website, says that pepper plants never seem to be nibbled by deer, and he favours the pepper spray. This may also help repel cats, but you have to remember to reapply it after rain. Finally, plant more than you need, and resign yourself to deer eating a portion of your produce. With increasing human intrusion into deer's natural habitat in the form of new suburbs, we can doubtless expect more frequent wildlife visits in the future (raccoons, deer, bear).

Raccoons

Even in the city, raccoons can be a problem. They are especially fond of corn and will use their dextrous fingers to open the husks. (Another reason to be leery of these animals if you have pets: raccoon urine is toxic to dogs.) When raccoons moved into our summer cottage for the winter, via the chimney, we were forced to confront these wily critters head on: we bought a live trap and removed seven of them to the woods 15 kilometres (9 miles) from the house, which is about the limit of their natural range. Make sure not to leave pet food or meat scraps lying around your yard to tempt raccoons; cute though they are, never feed them.

Slugs

Possibly one of the most revolting of garden predators, the slug is infamous for the slimy highways it secretes in the garden and along which it travels nightly en route to your plants. Slugs don't seem to be picky about their food, either—I once picked at least two dozen of them off my tomatoes, potatoes, beans, and small squash. (The prickles on the more mature cucumbers and squash seem to deter them; I haven't seen any signs of chewing on these, at least.) They seem to multiply in wet weather.

The most effective method of slug removal, as with potato bugs, is still hand picking—I know, they're slimy, but you can always wear gloves. When I was a kid, I was regularly sent into the garden patch after a rain with a tin full of salt to drop them in.

Unfortunately, mulch in the garden seems to attract slugs that appreciate the moist darkness underneath, especially during a hot season. Ruth Stout claims that her heavily mulched garden was not troubled by slugs since the mulch encouraged the proliferation of earthworms, whose castings (droppings) are alkaline and anathema to acid-loving slugs. Goodness knows I'm a fan of mulch, but my slugs, unlike Ruth's, don't seem bothered in the least by the worm poop.

Other slug deterrents you can try include sand, wood ash (especially the kind with sharp cinders in it), beer (in a saucer or tuna tin: the slugs crawl in and drown happy), and leaving certain weeds in the garden as an alternative food source. I've noticed that slugs seem to love the plantain that grows abundantly in the garden—it is all chewed up. I'm willing to live with this weed if they like it just as well as lettuce and beans.

The Organic Way to Plant Protection recommends strong soapy, sudsy water. Although I'm reluctant to dump lots of this on my vegetables—most soaps contain a fair amount of sodium, which can harm the soil—I would certainly try it in a slug-ridden flower bed.

Try laying old boards or shingles down among your plants; slugs will congregate under these on hot days to keep moist; you can then lift the boards up and remove the slugs or just step on the board to kill them.

Some gardeners recommend laying the remains of your morning grapefruit half, cut side down, in the garden; slugs will congregate under this citrus canopy and can then be collected and drowned.

Slugs ravaging a lettuce plant

Not all insects are intent on eating your crops; some are there to prey on other insects or pollinate your plants. Ladybugs, in particular, are great eaters of aphids, so much so that some organic gardeners will buy quantities of them to release directly into an infested area. Bees should always be welcomed, as many vegetables can't set fruit without their help in pollination. If your garden is overrun with spiders, don't run for cover—they are actually helping with insect control.

It's always a good idea to plant things that will attract beneficial insects. The authors of *The Urban Homestead* recommend planting a few of the following in your garden: plants from the cabbage, carrot, and sunflower family, as well as dill, clover, daisy, goldenrod, Queen Anne's lace, thyme, sweet alyssum, buckwheat, bee balm, cilantro, lovage, and/or parsley.

If you see a toad hopping through your veggie patch, thank your lucky stars: toads like to eat slugs. You can further encourage your resident amphibian by leaving an upturned clay flower pot in your garden as a toad house.

Gardener David McLearn tells me that ants like to eat slugs, so don't be so quick to kill these industrious critters if you spot them in the garden. (I've never heard of them eating plants.)

Weeds

Weeds are a fact of life for every gardener. These hardy, seemingly indestructible plants often flourish where you least want them and can take soil nutrients away from the vegetables you are trying to grow there. The silver lining of a weed infestation is that these plants can tell us something about the quality of our soil; they often act as Nature's remedial agents, restoring balance to soils. Many weeds are also edible and/or have valuable medicinal properties. For more detailed information on weedy delicacies, consult Szczawinski and Turner, *Edible Garden Weeds of Canada,* available at the public library. An informative website on the common weeds of the Northern United States and Canada is maintained by the Canadian Weed Science Society (weedscience.ca). This site provides photos and botanical descriptions of the weeds you may encounter in your garden which will help you with identification.

Diagnostic weeds

Some weeds grow in a variety of soil types (dandelions are a ubiquitous example). Look for large populations of a single species of weed rather than a few individuals as a clue to soil type or condition.

FERTILE SOIL (lots of manure and compost added): Lamb's quarter, chickweed, chicory, thistles, plantain, mallow, and dandelions. (Dandelions actually produce humus; having them in your garden or lawn indicates good soil quality.)

COMPACTED SOIL (common if your soil is clayey rather than sandy): Plantain, horse nettle, knotweed, quack grass.

ACIDIC SOIL: Moss, plantain, sorrel, daisy, knotweed, horsetail.

ALKALINE SOIL: Clover, Queen Anne's lace, chicory, chickweed.

Spring in Nova Scotia means the return of the cheerful dandelion.

Clover

There's a reason cows and rabbits love this plant: the flowers, when pulled apart, are sweet and delicious. Your pet rodent will also love both the flowers and the leaves of the clover.

Dandelion

I've seen dandelion greens sold for several dollars a bag at health-food stores in the early spring. Why not pick some on your very own lawn? Actually, many parts of the dandelion plant are edible, though somewhat bitter. The root can be roasted and made into a coffee substitute that is also sold in health-food stores.

Clover is a sweet treat, and not just for rabbits!

I was very happy to discover recently that the village of Wallace on Nova Scotia's North Shore has begun hosting an annual dandelion festival in late May, featuring dandelion root-beer tasting and lawn-mower racing, among other activities. What a great way to celebrate spring!

Lamb's Quarter
If you use manure or compost, you will likely encounter this heavy-feeding weed that is a dead ringer for spinach in taste and nutrients. Pick it when it is still small and steam it for 2 to 5 minutes for a delicious side dish, or use like spinach in quiches, curries, soups, or spanakopitas.

Invasive weeds

Of course, we can't always eat our way to a weedless garden. Some invasives like goutweed and Japanese knotweed may quickly become an infestation unless rooted out or smothered: throw cardboard, a piece of old carpet, black plastic, or any material that blocks sunlight on top of a weedy patch to kill them.

The best way to deal with most other kinds of weeds is to root them out before they go to seed, and chuck them on the compost pile for next year's humus. I find weeding a very relaxing activity; if you haven't done it for a while, the results will be dramatic and satisfying.

If you're truly not keen on weeding, you can mulch your plants heavily using straw, hay, grass clippings, leaves, or eelgrass. (Don't cover up your vegetables in the process!) Keep the bare pathways well-mulched too; in a dry summer, mulching will help to keep the moisture in, which will reduce the amount of watering you have to do.

While most of us have looked with longing at catalogue photos of immaculate gardens with nary a weed nor insect-bitten plant to be seen, it is important to realize that achieving this look comes at a cost. With our increasing knowledge of the dangers of chemical pesticides, especially to children and pets, we need to reevaluate our priorities as gardeners. Most of us would be willing to accept a few weeds as a normal part of gardening.

As for the critters that call our gardens home, expert grower Marjorie Willison reminds us in her comprehensive *East Coast Gardener* that "the best defence against insects is fertile, well-drained soil with plenty of organic matter and adequate moisture; healthy plants are less likely to attract insects and are better able to continue growing and developing if harmful insects do attack. One could view insect damage early in the season as a sort of pruning as healthy plants respond with more, healthy growth." Sage advice indeed.

CHAPTER 8

Preserving the Harvest: Tips and Techniques

Something I call fall fever comes over me in late August and early September; perhaps it is the shortening days and cool evenings that effect a metamorphosis from gardener to pickler. Like many throwbacks to a former age, I go into overdrive collecting and preserving the fruits (and vegetables) of my labours—a daunting process as things are often ripening all at once. The preserving instinct is something of a bitter irony in our Canadian climate: just as the weather is at its warmest and we are most tempted to be outdoors, the ripe fruits of this warm season conspire to tether us to our kitchens, turning it all into jams, jellies, pickles, and relishes to sustain us through the coming winter months. Ripe vegetables wait for no one.

Until quite recently, root crops were the only vegetables eaten through the long Nova Scotian winters, with the exception of the pickles and relishes made of poor keepers like cucumbers and tomatoes. With oil and food prices steadily rising, it seems conceivable that we will someday return to the way our grandparents ate: that is, locally and in season.

In earlier generations, the arrival of seasonal fruits and vegetables was an occasion to be celebrated to the orgy point: the twice-daily strawberry shortcake diet that gave my grandfather a case of hives one July. Or the ripe tomatoes whose acidic juices swelled my great-grandfather's gums every summer so that his false teeth no longer fit him—when this happened, he would simply toss the teeth into a drawer and "gum it" until the end of the tomato season.

There are many ways to enjoy the harvest besides eating it all at once. Freezing and jelly-making are the most common preserving methods for whole fruit. For vegetables, there are also many options, depending on the vegetable, such as pickling, canning, freezing, or cold storing (root cellaring). What follows are a few suggestions.

Preserves await their moment on the dinner table.

The Root Cellar

An evocative place name, calling up images of damp, earthy coolness, the root cellar is a time-honoured method of keeping root crops cool for their long winter hibernation. Keeping produce in a cool place below the frost line (the depth below which the ground doesn't freeze—around 1.2 metres or 4 feet) slows fruits' and vegetables' ripening processes as well as holding off the spread of bacterial and fungal rot, in a way similar to a refrigerator. Unlike a refrigerator, though, a root cellar requires no electricity and little to no money to build. In fact, root cellar-like conditions may already exist in your house. You are especially lucky if you have an unheated basement; potatoes, carrots, turnips, and beets can live happily there for several months in slatted wooden crates or bushel baskets (the slats will allow air to circulate among the veggies). Some people insulate a portion of their garage to store root crops for the winter.

An excellent print resource for constructing a wide variety of both simple and elaborate root cellars is *Root Cellaring: Natural Cold Storage of Fruits and Vegetables* by Mike and Nancy Bubel, a book that should be available at most libraries. These pros offer a number of tips on winter vegetable storage.

Choose well-formed, healthy, unblemished produce to store. Even small blemishes can be an entry point for bacteria that can spoil surrounding vegetables.

Keep in mind that some veggies require curing before being stored: onions and garlic are a good example. You should dry these on a raised rack. The Bubels recommend 3 to 7 drying days. Squash and pumpkins (with the exception of acorn squash) need 10 to 14 days to cure at room temperature before being placed in a cooler place; a root cellar is too damp and cold for these cucurbits, so try something drier, like an attic or heated basement (don't put vegetables near a working furnace).

As noted above, not all vegetables need the same storage conditions. Some require higher or lower temperatures and humidity levels.

Expect some spoilage, even under ideal conditions. Don't worry too much about this—just add it to the compost pile and think of it as food for next year's crop.

Canning

Long before refrigeration, canning was the only way to preserve the season's perishable fruits, vegetables, and some meats. The safest methods for canning, according to the authors of *Putting Food By,* are the boiling-water bath (for high-acid foods like pickles and tomato sauces) and pressure canning (for low-acid foods: most vegetables, meat, and seafood). I highly recommend consulting this valuable text if you're contemplating canning—it gives detailed instructions for safe home-preserving methods for all kinds of food. I've put down hundreds of cans of food in my lifetime, always using the boiling water–bath technique. I've always been jittery around pressure-canners and cookers, but that's just my own nervous disposition—the authors of *Putting Food By* give great advice on how to use this tool successfully and safely.

Why are these processes necessary?

In a nutshell, the boiling-water bath and pressure-cooking techniques kill all the yeasts, molds, and bacteria that cause spoilage inside food containers. Some of these bacteria—such as the ones that cause botulism—are deadly and can grow in the absence of air (inside of your jar!), so you don't want to take any chances. The boiling-water bath and pressure-canning also create a vacuum inside food jars that allows the jars to seal themselves, keeping airborne spoilage at bay.

There is a science behind proper canning that starts with having the right tools at your disposal. Your canning pot needs to be deep enough to allow 2.5–5 centimetres (1–2 inches) of boiling water to cover your jars without slopping over the sides. (A cheap stainless steel stockpot works well and doesn't take up much space on top of your stove.) You'll also need a rack for the jars to sit on inside the canner (I use a circular cooling rack for cookies); when the water is really boiling, jars sitting directly on the bottom of the canner jump around like hot potatoes and may even break. You'll also need a pair of tongs or a heat-resistant silicone glove to lift the jars out of the canner.

One of the best investments you'll ever make as a home preserver is the humble Mason jar (or Bell jar, or any other home canning bottle). These sturdy bottles come in a variety of sizes and shapes: look for them throughout the year at hardware and department stores, and specifically around midsummer in most grocery stores. Whatever bottle you choose, you'll need the right lid and screw band for it: most sizes of Mason jar have a one-size-fits-all lid and screw band, although some wide-mouth jars will take a larger lid. You'll notice that the inside of the lid has a rubber ring around it that creates the vacuum seal necessary to keep food inside from spoiling.

Some tools of the canning trade: Mason jars and lids, a corn boiler, and tongs.

Golden brandy peaches

When the lid has been used once for canning, *it cannot be used a second time for that purpose.* I mark old lids with an "x" with an indelible marker and continue to use them with my Mason jars to store food in the fridge, though. Screw bands are fine to use again for canning as long as they're not rusty. You'll need to buy a new set of lids each year for canning, but they cost only a few dollars.

Whatever you're canning, it's important to leave enough headroom at the top of the jar: most recipes recommend at least 1.5 centimetres (½ inch) of headroom, but I usually make it 2.5 centimetres (1 inch), just to be safe. Always use clean jars and fresh lids.

Most recipes for pickles, relishes, jams, and jellies will specify the length of time required in the boiling-water bath: typically, 10 to 15 minutes for standard pint jars.

High-acid foods like lemons, oranges, strawberries, some apples, raspberries, plums, and gooseberries are natural choices for home-canned jams, jellies, and marmalades. Some tomato varieties have been hybridized to have lower acidity and so should be canned with caution. To increase the acidity of your tomato sauces, add vinegar or citric acid (though be warned that these acidifying agents can give food an unpleasantly astringent taste).

BRANDY PEACHES

Peaches are a fruit that, like apples, taste as good cooked as they do raw. I'm including a delicious peach preserve for you to try, even if the peaches may not the fruit of your own labours. I encourage anyone with the space to plant a peach tree, and otherwise, head to a U-Pick or a farmers' market and load up with this wonderful local delicacy. The Annapolis Valley has its peach peak in late summer, just about the time when you'll be least tempted to spend an afternoon in the kitchen standing over a hot stove. The flavour of these peaches, however, is worth the effort; they are delicious on plain yogurt, vanilla ice cream, in fruit salads, or as a crepe filling, and their lovely golden colour will remind you of late August when you pull them off the shelf on a cold winter day.

Peel peaches by submerging them in boiling water until their skins start to loosen, then in cold water so they won't burn your fingers while you're peeling them.

Any number of peaches will work here, but you'll need to make syrup to can them with: for every 1 pound (454 grams) of peaches, you'll need 1 cup (250 millilitres) of sugar and 1 cup (250 millilitres) of water. Boil sugar and water. At this point, I like to add about ¼ teaspoon (1 millilitre) of ascorbic acid to the syrup, which will keep the peaches from darkening like apples do when they're peeled. (You can buy ascorbic acid at most health-food stores, or crush up a Vitamin C tablet to add to the syrup.)

Pack peaches in clean pint or quart jars, adding 2 tablespoons (30 millilitres) of brandy to each pint (0.5 litres), or 4 tablespoons (60 millilitres) per quart (1.1 litres). Fill the jars with syrup, leaving ½ inch (about 1.5 centimetres) of headroom and adjust lids.

Process jars in a boiling-water bath for 20 minutes (pints) or 2 minutes (quarts).

Remove jars, being careful not to tighten screw bands which will break the seal. As they cool, listen for the telltale "pop" made as the lids vacuum seal themselves. You'll be able to tell that they've sealed by looking for a slight concavity to each lid.

Pickling

A preserving method often used in conjunction with canning to ensure food safety, pickling involves adding generous amounts of salt to vegetables to cure them against spoilage. The old-fashioned ceramic crocks used to hold the winter's supply of pickles were, of course, not sealed or heat-processed: the acidity of

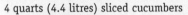

Bread-and-butter pickles

BREAD-AND-BUTTER PICKLES

This classic sweet and crunchy pickle goes well with everything from sandwiches to stews.

4 quarts (4.4 litres) sliced cucumbers
6 medium onions
⅓ cup (75 millilitres) pickling salt (table salt is iodized and can discolour vegetables
   when used for pickling)

Submerge the above ingredients in a bowl of water and ice cubes and allow to sit for 3 hours. Drain well.

Meanwhile, in a saucepan, bring to a boil for 2 minutes:
3 cups (750 millilitres) of white sugar
1½ teaspoons (7 millilitres) turmeric
1½ teaspoons (7 millilitres) celery seed
2 tablespoons (30 millilitres) mustard seed
3 cups (750 millilitres) cider vinegar

Add soaked vegetables to liquid and bring to a low boil for a minute or two. Pack in clean jars and top with hot lids; process in boiling-water bath for 10 minutes. Remove and cool. These pickles improve in flavour after "steeping" for a few weeks.

the vinegar and the preservative aspect of the salt made pickles an inhospitable place for most bacteria. My grandmother and many of her generation never heat-processed any of their homemade pickles (cooking cucumbers can make them somewhat mushy), but it's better to be safe than sorry, so go ahead and dunk those dills and bread-and-butters in a boiling-water bath anyway.

KETCHUP
(from the *Boston Cooking School Cookbook*)

Impress your friends with a tangy substitute for the store-bought squeeze bottle. One of my favourite parts of autumn is the pungent scent of this ketchup simmering on the back of the stove; it takes a long time to cook, so wait for a chilly day or visit a friend with a woodstove.

Ingredients
8 quarts (8.8 litres) ripe tomatoes
¼ cup (50 millilitres) pickling salt
2 cups (500 millilitres) white sugar
1 tablespoon (15 millilitres) cayenne pepper
1 tablespoon (15 millilitres) mace
1 tablespoon (15 millilitres) celery seed
2 tablespoons (30 millilitres) cinnamon
2 quarts (2.2 litres) vinegar

Cut tomatoes in pieces, add other ingredients, and cook slowly until reduced by half (about 2 hours). Strain, reheat, and seal (use a boiling-water bath for 15 minutes). If desired, add 6 cloves of garlic with spices.

Makes 2 to 3 quarts (about 2 to 3 litres) of ketchup.

GREEN TOMATO MINCEMEAT

A different version of the traditional Christmas pie filling; great for using up green tomatoes, and it freezes well.

Ingredients

2 quarts (2.2 litres) green tomatoes
10 tart apples
1 cup (250 millilitres) suet
1 cup (250 millilitres) vinegar
2½ cups (625 millilitres) brown sugar
1 cup (250 millilitres) mixed peel
½ cup (125 millilitres) molasses
1½ teaspoons (7 millilitres) cinnamon
1 teaspoon (5 millilitres) ground cloves
1 teaspoon (5 millilitres) nutmeg
1 teaspoon (5 millilitres) salt
the juice and rind of 1 orange and 1 lemon
1 pound (0.454 kilograms) raisins

Chop tomatoes. Cover with boiling water and boil for 20 minutes; drain. Add apples and other ingredients and boil slowly for 1.5 hours.

Add to pie shell and bake until crust is golden brown, or freeze mincemeat in plastic yogourt containers for next Christmas.

Green tomato mincemeat can be frozen or canned.

DILLY (PICKLED) BEANS

I discovered these the year my cucumbers failed and I couldn't make dill pickles. Carrots, sliced lengthwise, would also work well.

The heat-processing times (and recipe) come from *Putting Food By,* the bible of canning and preserving.

Ingredients

2 pounds (about 1 kilogram) whole green beans
4 fresh dill heads or 1 teaspoon dried dill seed
4 cloves of garlic, peeled
2½ cups (625 millilitres) vinegar
2½ cups (625 millilitres) water
about ¼ cup (50 millilitres) of pickling salt (non-iodized)

Wash beans, removing stems and tips—cut into uniform lengths to allow beans to stand upright in pint jars; don't let them go higher than the "shoulder" of the jar.

Jars should be clean and very hot. Have lids and sealers ready in scalding water. Each jar gets a dill head and a garlic clove. Pack beans in jars, leaving 1 inch (3 centimetres) of headroom.

Heat together the water, vinegar, and salt: when it boils, pour over the beans, filling each jar to ½ inch (1.5 centimetres) from the top. Run a plastic knife down and around to remove trapped air, adjust lids, and process in a boiling-water bath for 10 minutes after water in canner returns to simmer. Remove jars and listen for the popping sounds of the lids as they cool.

Blanching and freezing

Just about any vegetable can be frozen successfully, that is, be able to spend several months in your freezer and emerge with some semblance of its original taste and texture intact. The key to freezing veggies is blanching, also known as partial pre-cooking. This process halts the enzymes in your vegetables that make them lose flavour and colour, even when they're frozen. To blanch veggies, simply dunk your prepared vegetable into boiling water for a few minutes, then immediately transfer it to ice water for the same amount of time. Blanched vegetables can then be drained and put into a freezer bag or yogourt container. (I find glass bottles don't work well: too many have smashed in the freezer or shortly after I took them out.) If you're using freezer bags, use a drinking straw to suck the air out of each bag before sealing it up with a twist-tie (a

FROZEN BEANS

Beans are good candidates for preserving. If you've planted more than a few bushes or poles, you may find yourself overwhelmed and tired of eating them when they're at their best in summer. Frozen beans are great for tossing into a soup or using as a side dish.

Get a large pot of water boiling, and after having removed the stems and tips from your beans (and chopping them into pieces, if you wish), submerge them in the boiling water for 3 minutes. Remove them and plunge them into a large bowl of ice water for 3 more minutes.

If you don't want your beans to develop a rust (brownish discolouration on the pod), it's a good idea to dry them off after blanching, using a large bath towel. I like to roll small batches of beans up in the towel to remove the moisture.

My grandfather's drying method involved the spin cycle of the washing machine: he would pour the blanched beans into an old, clean pillowcase, tie the end off, and let the washer spin them for about 2 minutes. It really worked!

When the beans are dry, you can freeze them in plastic freezer bags or Ziploc bags; use a straw to suck the air out of each bag before sealing it. This will keep the beans tasting fresh.

version of vacuum packing that will keep vegetables tasting fresher longer).

You can buy pots that have built-in baskets for cooking vegetables—this will make fishing pieces of veggie out of the boiling water more expeditious. If you don't have a basket, you can tie your vegetables into cheesecloth and submerge the whole bundle into the boiling pot. *Putting Food By* contains a useful list of boiling times for many different vegetables; smaller ones (or pieces) take less time than big pieces—the range is 1½ to 4 minutes.

The recipes included in this chapter are ones that, for me, embody the delights of Nova Scotia's autumn, its mingled sweet and tart flavours looking back to the warmth of summer and ahead to the chill of winter. They vividly remind me of happy times spent with my grandparents in their kitchen, all of us working hard to put down the summer's harvest. For me, there are few pleasures greater than looking at jars of pickles made from homegrown vegetables. I think you'll agree that the wonderful flavours of these preserves make them worth the extra effort.

CHAPTER 9

Farmer Mentors of Nova Scotia

Though we may occasionally dream of a lush expanse of fertile farmland on which to grow plentiful produce, many city dwellers are faced with the hard reality of cramped backyards or small apartment balconies on which to grow our vegetables. Other would-be urban farmers may be averse to digging up tulip beds and cutting down lilac bushes to accommodate their edibles. And then there's our ever-changing Maritime weather to contend with. Whether they live in the city or the country, most gardeners will experience setbacks throughout the growing season, some of them serious enough to make us want to give up the whole enterprise.

With the hope that I might inspire you to overcome some of the common obstacles to gardening, I have included the stories of some intrepid individuals living in both rural and urban Nova Scotia settings who have accepted the challenges of growing food on both small and large scales, with delicious results. The growers profiled here reflect the several geographic areas of the province as well as some interesting recent trends in vegetable gardening.

David McLearn: Vegetables on city property, exposed!

City of Halifax gardener David McLearn quietly embodies the spirit of sustainable urban food production. He's been tending the city's flower beds for the past twenty-four years. Only in the past decade has he begun sneaking vegetables in among the familiar summer annuals, a practice he says city officials didn't notice at first, though after a newspaper article about the Upper Kennetcook native appeared in the *Community Herald* last fall, David's secret was definitely out. He won a Halifax Regional Municipality (HRM) Director's Award and a Chief Administrative Officer (CAO) award last year for his work in the city's gardens, proof that being subversive sometimes pays off!

At HRM's Cowie Hill property last fall, stately cornstalks were flanked by cheerful

David McLearn transplants kale at a city-owned garden plot.

yellow marigolds and Scarlet Runner beans climbed the chain-link fence, their bright red blossoms drawing the bees. A zucchini flower peeked out between the snapdragons on a side hill.

When I met David, he and a helper were hard

at work on two large beds at Conrose Field that will be dedicated to vegetables. Garlics planted last fall occupy the central portion of the bed, interspersed with Brussels sprouts and pole beans, which will eventually climb the stalks of the sprouts. A border of purplish kale was being planted as we spoke. The transplants were started in city greenhouses and will be planted in other city-owned beds.

"I have two beds at St. Mary's Boat Club, two at Conrose, five at Centennial Park in Bedford, and three at Cowie Hill," he recounts while heeling in a kale plant.

Some favourite crops of David's are rainbow Swiss chard, whose colourful stalks add an ornamental flair to any garden, along with red mustard, golden beets ("they're sweeter than the red ones and don't bleed when you boil them"), and rainbow carrots.

Scarlet Runner beans decorate this Cowie Hill chain-link fence.

David estimated that last year, he gave away more than two hundred grocery bags of produce to Hope Cottage and hopes for more of the same this season. (The food bank doesn't usually accept fresh produce.)

I ask David what plant varieties don't mind

Halifax's sometimes foggy, cool summers: "Kale, cabbage, and Brussels sprouts are good; onions and garlic don't mind the wet."

When it comes to food, David believes that cities should become far more self-sufficient; he gestures towards Conrose's expanse of unbroken lawn as an example—and I can almost see him planning his pole-bean patch next to the climbing bars on the playground. His own creative use of existing ornamental beds is a timely reminder that even a small patch of ground can yield delightful results.

Susan Kerslake: Balcony gardening in the heart of the city

Not every gardener has the luxury of a sunny backyard—or any backyard, for that matter. Gardener Susan Kerslake lives on the fourth floor of a downtown Halifax apartment building and has been growing flowers, vegetables, and even trees on her two-by-three-metre balcony for nine years (and for the twenty-two years before that at her previous apartment). "I call it 'the forest and the farm,'" says Susan with a smile as we gaze out past the leafy Norway maple and poplar growing in large tubs on the balcony floor. In winter, she insulates them against the cold with bags of leaves; when the trees outgrow the confines of the balcony, Susan will give them away to friends with a backyard.

In summer, Susan's "forest" is joined by a variety of vegetables and flowers. An assortment of five-litre plastic food containers with drilled drainage holes act as planters. A consistent triumph of Susan's has been Scarlet Runner beans, which swing on long strings suspended from her sympathetic upstairs neighbour's balcony like a lush, green curtain. To grow them, "all you need is a bucket, soil, and seed," says Susan. "If every person in the building had a bucket of Scarlet Runners, this place would look like Europe."

Susan's choice of vegetables for her balcony is determined by two factors: wind

TIPS FROM DAVID MCLEARN

Use a thick layer of leaves underneath your topsoil as a slow-release fertilizer; worms will do the work of breaking down the leaves into valuable compost that will feed your plants throughout the growing season.

Use more compost and less peat in containers to keep moisture in—remember that potted outdoor plants need more watering than those planted directly into the soil.

Trellised sweet peas enjoy the view from the fourth floor.

and space. Some plants are put off by the steady breezes on her south-facing balcony, which Susan says also gets too hot to grow lettuce. She gave up growing cucumbers, famous for their sprawl: "I didn't like the feeling of hairy leaves over my shoulder." Every year she buys a well-established patio tomato from a greenhouse for her garden; other choices are dictated by her two pet guinea pigs who enjoy munching on the rye grass and oats she grows for them around the base of the two trees. As a renter, Susan knows it's important to keep things tidy on the balcony; she notes that not all apartment buildings allow balcony gardens.

The two most important qualities of a balcony gardener, according to Susan, are "patience and curiosity. Being curious and not counting on it to work out. Every

An assortment of flowers and vegetables grow on Susan Kerslake's balcony.

year, it's different; some years are better for some vegetables." Her advice applies just as much to earth-bound gardeners as to their elevated counterparts.

Friends in high places: high-rise gardening

If you plan to turn your apartment balcony into a green oasis, it's best to check with your superintendent to make sure building rules governing external appearance allow for gardens.

Depending on the age and condition of your building and the materials used in constructing its balconies, you might also want to consider what potential strain many tubs of garden soil might have on the structure. Most buildings use reinforced concrete rather than wood in balcony construction, so you should be fine.

Be a responsible balcony gardener and minimize the risk of your pots blowing off the balcony: set them on the floor. Don't leave pots on ledges, and avoid hanging baskets and window boxes.

Container gardening

There are many advantages to this kind of gardening. The soil in containers warms up quickly—a boon for heat-loving plants like tomatoes. You can control what kind of soil gets added to your containers, and they are portable: you can move them into a sunny patch and bring them inside on cold nights. You can grow almost any variety of vegetable you want in a container, provided that container is big enough.

Your choice of containers is limited only by your imagination. I've seen discarded plastic milk crates "repurposed" into plant containers. They drain really well and you can line up groups of them into nice, symmetrical vegetable beds—especially handy for those whose sunniest piece of property is an asphalt or gravel-covered driveway. If soil starts to sift out through the holes in the crates, you can line them with cardboard or permeable fabric cloth, available at hardware stores and garden centres.

If you're taking a road trip this summer and stop at an ice-cream stand, why not ask if you can have some of those big tubs? Some vendors will ask for fifty cents for them;

A really good resource for would-be apartment gardeners is the Toronto-based website *Toronto Balconies Bloom* (torontobalconiesbloom. ca). This site contains photographs of all kinds of multi-storey balcony gardens, from the shady north-facing to the full-sun south-facing, along with inspiring stories and tips from the owners who love them. A balcony-growing tip from Toronto apartment gardener Marco Pagliarulo: Plant the same seeds in different areas of your balcony to see where each grows best.

others might give them away. Make sure to drill drainage holes in the bottom of your new planters.

Many folks throw away large plant pots—most of them plastic, but the occasional clay one will turn up. If you rescue them, make sure to clean them well with dish soap and water in case the previous occupant was sick—some plant diseases can linger in soil and pots. Don't use antibacterial soaps containing triclosan, which has been shown to be persistent in the environment and may kill beneficial soil bacteria

Vertical gardening: the ultimate in space saving

Relatively new in the gardening scene is the upside-down hanging planter (close cousin to the hanging bag; literally, a long, heavy-duty plastic bag with holes poked in for plants to grow through). This kind of design allows you to suspend your tomato, pepper, cucumber, or other fruiting plant from the side of your house, garage, or tree branch. You can buy these contraptions, or make your own by cutting a hole in the bottom of a coir-lined hanging basket liner—the kind usually used for flowers. Take your transplant and feed its root ball and the bottom part of its stem up through the hole from the outside. Pack in some good-quality potting soil around the root and there you have it—ready to hang! Don't forget to water it.

Jean Snow and Bob Kropla: A new twist on the family farm

You might never know it to look at their Dartmouth house, but Jean Snow and her husband Bob Kropla are urban farmers. The backyard at Bob and Jean's, the nucleus of their Lake City Farm business, is largely under cultivation; the main crop is salad greens, along with a changing assortment of other edibles such as turnips, tomatoes, onions, peppers, and cucumbers. Lake City's salad mixes were a big hit at last year's Dartmouth Farmers' Market, and at several local grocery stores, which was a great encouragement to the first-time urban farmers. This year, they have expanded their territory through a relatively new practice known as "backyard sharing": two nearby Dartmouth households have loaned their yards to Jean and Bob in exchange for a share

Bob Kropla at Lake City Farm's open house in August

of the produce. One of these properties has a garden bed measuring 15 metres by 21 metres (50 feet by 70 feet)—that's a lot of salad! Property owners must provide a water supply for the garden and must do their own composting.

Lake City Farm uses the principles of small plot intensive (SPIN) farming, ideally suited to an urban environment where space is at a premium. They don't bother with ploughing up the lawn; instead, they use the sheet composting (lasagna gardening) method of building

Jean Snow creates a microclimate for her seedlings on the back deck of the family house.

up soil layers on top of the existing lawn, starting with a cardboard layer and adding peat moss, composted manure, leaves, and other organic materials. This method has worked especially well for their greens, which have fairly shallow roots.

Building on last year's success, Lake City Farm will inaugurate a weekly box program to a small number of customers this season; a form of consumer-supported agriculture that is becoming popular among urban dwellers who don't garden them-

Another recent phenomenon in the gardening world is landsharing, a practice that pairs enthusiastic would-be gardeners who lack space for their enterprises with non-gardening property owners who would like to see their yards used for cultivation. No money exchanges hands, though landowners are often offered a portion of the produce grown on their land. Using the latest Google mapping technology to advertise available space, new landshares are popping up in cities all over Canada: for information on the Halifax version, visit ecologyaction.ca/content/halifax-landshare.

selves, but who want to enjoy the benefits of fresh local produce throughout the growing season. At twenty dollars per week, the contents of the box will depend on what's growing that week on the farm.

Bob and Jean's non-conventional experiment proves that farms can exist in the city—even without the livestock.

For more information on Lake City Farm, go to their website at lakecityfarm.com or email lakecityfarm@eastlink.ca.

Lake City Farms "borrows" space, including this Dartmouth garden plot, for its operation from nearby property owners.

Community gardening at university: the SeeMore Green experience

The Seymour (or SeeMore) Green Community Garden, tucked away behind the old History Department on the Dalhousie University campus, started life in 1996 through the good offices of NSPIRG (the Nova Scotia Public Interest Research Group) and the efforts of Jen Scott and Wayne Grosko. It first occupied a vacant lot owned by the Department of Facilities Management at 1443 Seymour Street, but had to move when the space was needed for a new building. Its new location, though shady, features a shed with a green roof built in 2005 (prior to this, a group of Dal architecture students had built a straw bale shed on the site), and several raised beds, made from recycled materials, that house shade-tolerant produce, herbs, and medicinal weeds, as well as a cob oven for barbecues during the growing season. Students who tend SeeMore Green use the greenhouse at the nearby Life Sciences building to start their seeds before transplanting them into the outdoor garden.

This community project receives funding for a summer student to coordinate activities at the garden; I spoke with the 2006–07 coordinator, Jayme Melrose, now a graduate of Dalhousie's Community Design program, who spoke fondly of her time at SeeMore Green. In addition to regular garden work parties, workshops held at the Green over the past few years have covered diverse topics such as seed saving, worm (and regular) composting, medicinal and edible weeds, an introduction to permaculture, and building your own bike trailer.

Community gardens in HRM

If you live in Halifax and don't have space for a garden, joining a community garden may be the way to go. There are a few groups in operation in and around the city as of this writing (not a complete list, I'm sure).

- The Peninsula Urban Gardens Society (PUGS, formerly the North End Community Gardens Association) was founded in 1999 to promote urban agriculture and community development. They currently operate at two locations: Prescott Street in Halifax's North End, and Gorsebrook Gardens, behind Century Towers on Wellington Street (South End). For around twenty dollars, you can rent a 5-square-metre (64-quare-foot) garden plot, seeds, access to water, and veggie-growing advice. Check their website at pugs.chebucto.org.

- The Dartmouth Gardening Association has recently started up a new community garden at the Findlay Centre, 26 Elliott Street, Dartmouth, with plots for rent to the community (contact goodnessgrowsdartmouth@gmail.com for more information).
- The Halifax Christian Church in Clayton Park West is now operating a community garden and is looking for volunteers to help tend it. Contact the church directly for more information.
- I've heard rumours recently about a community garden being established next to the new Mainland Common Community Centre in Clayton Park West. Let's hope it gets going, since there must be plenty of green-thumbed apartment dwellers in that area who could use the space.

Joanna Brown: the Urban Farm Museum Society of Spryfield

The community of Spryfield was once Halifax's bread basket, beginning in the late eighteenth century, when Captain William Spry, Chief Military Engineer for Nova Scotia, cleared his 1,000 acres (405 hectares) of land on the other side of the Northwest Arm and, in turn, made way for a thriving farming community in Spryfield. At least five dairies in the area supplied Halifax with its milk during the nineteenth and early twentieth centuries, but by the 1960s, the last Spryfield farm had ceased production, ending a generations-old way of life and increasing the city's dependence on imported food.

William Kidston bought part of the original Spry farmland in 1822—"by 1827, Kidston's Thornhill Farm, later renamed Rockingstone Farm, was

Volunteers hard at work at the Spryfield Urban Farm Museum

producing wheat, mixed grains, potatoes and hay, and supported cattle, horses, pigs and sheep on 30 cleared acres" (Urban Farm Museum Society of Spryfield brochure). As late as the 1930s, descendant John Kidston was raising chickens and squab (young pigeons) for the kitchens of Halifax hotels, as well as supplying eggs, rabbits, hay, and vegetables. His daughter Janet continues to live in the old Kidston farmhouse, which today is a bed and breakfast.

It was a sad day for the family—and, in many ways, for the city—when most of the Kidstons' farmland was expropriated in 1969 to make way for housing development, an act which threatened to eclipse nearly two hundred years of agricultural activity on the site.

Fortunately, one of the remaining Kidston fields was spared and today is licensed to the Urban Farm Museum Society of Spryfield, an organization dedicated, in its own words, "to the commemoration of the area's agricultural heritage, to the facilitation of food production in the urban area, to the education of local schoolchildren in natural and social sciences, the arts and home economics, and to strengthening the traditional social fabric of Spryfield."

The Kidston homestead dates from the 1820s.

Spearheaded in 1996 by MLA Michele Raymond, Pat MacLean, and master gardener Marjorie Willison, all of whom have a connection to Spryfield, the organization hosts picnics, plant sales, and heritage walks as well as outdoor evening concerts in the summer, and a harvest fair in September. Their cookbook, *Foods of Spry's Field,* is also a guide to the preserving arts of bygone times. The success of the group is attested to by an ambitious new project— a second collective garden project at Greystone, now in its fourth year—and a 2007 Lieutenant Governor's Award.

The garden serves as a gathering place for volunteers who come every Thursday morning throughout the summer to work in the large raised vegetable gardens— some beds are dedicated market gardens, growing produce that the group sells at the farm gate, while others are reserved for community children who come on Saturday mornings to practice growing vegetables. The grounds of the farm are a peaceful oasis, shrouded from surrounding suburban homes by a thick border of trees. Coming to the garden is like stepping back in time—if you disregard the lack of livestock, this could be the eighteenth century.

Joanna Brown, who is a paid gardener at the Urban Farm, talks to me while pulling weeds from a raised bed. She explains that the farm keeps a few private plots for members of the community to use, but that most of the plots are gardened collectively. A portion of each year's harvest is given to hard-working volunteers. I ask her what vegetables are the most popular at the farm: pumpkins, corn, peas, beans, and basil top the list.

Is there much vandalism at the farm?

"Some," says Joanna, "but once the local kids start working here, there's less." Janet Kidston, descendant of the farm's original owner, agrees. Most kids who have come to the farm seem to feel protective towards it. The afterhours teenagers who sometimes come to drink at the secluded farm's picnic table are often treated to a friendly visit from Janet, "just out to work in the garden." The mother of two former teenagers herself, Janet smiles wickedly as she says, "They don't usually stay after that!"

For more information on the Urban Farm Museum Society of Spryfield and its projects, call 477-6087 or check their website: urbanfarmspryfield.com.

Owen Bridge: Annapolis Seeds

It is hard to believe that Owen Bridge, proprietor of Annapolis Seeds, is only seventeen years old. The knowledgeable young farmer and entrepreneur from Nictaux, just outside Middleton, Nova Scotia, began his heritage seed business in the fall of 2008, though his interest in gardening goes back much further, to the time when Owen and his family lived in Qualicum Beach on Vancouver Island. As Owen recounts, "When I was about ten years old, I met Dan Jason from Salt Spring Seeds; he really inspired me to go into seed saving, growing and preserving these heritage varieties. Because I was home-schooled, I could do as much research as I wanted, so I decided to spend all my time researching vegetable growing, organic farming, and all sorts of related stuff. It became my passion."

Prohibitive land prices on the West Coast drove the Bridge family east to where farmland was more affordable; they bought their thirty-five-hectare Nictaux property

Owen Bridge and his millet crop

in 2006. My late summer visit to the farm reveals a tranquil scene: several heritage Buff Orpington hens stroll serenely around the gardens and a pair of goats bleat inquisitively from a small barn. Bessie the Jersey cow nurses her new calf, Sally, in the back pasture. The comfortable house dates from the 1850s and serves as Owen's company headquarters. Visitors can buy seed at the door for three dollars a packet, although the bulk of his sales are made via the Internet. Having completely sold out of stock last year, Owen has quadrupled his seed-growing capacity this season; he attributes the success of the fledgling company to many folks' new-found concerns about peak energy and imported food, and their desire for greater self-sufficiency.

Most of the work of growing and harvesting the vegetables for their seed is done by Owen himself, though he gets occasional help from volunteers on the WWOOF program (World Wide Opportunities on Organic Farms), as well as from his seven-year-old brother Colin, who proudly shows me the medal he won at a recent scything competition in New Ross. As the Bridge boys' proficiency with the scythe would suggest, a good deal of the work on the farm is done by hand, from the milking of the cow to the cutting of grain. Inside the 1880s-era barn, several dozen varieties of newly harvested pea

Owen's dryer is a faster way to dry peas and beans.

pods, next year's seed stock, are being dried in hammocks pinned to the rafters. The bean crop is the next to be brought in: last year's bestselling variety, Lazy Housewife, dates from the early 1800s, when it gained popularity among married women as one of the first stringless bean varieties on the market.

Not all of Owen's varieties could be called true heirlooms (that is, predating World War Two), though all are open-pollinated, in keeping with Owen's interest in seeing his customers save seed to grow again. "It's about keeping all this biodiversity alive—not just that, but expanding on it, developing new strains and varieties as they pop up." Owen's keen eye sometimes catches an interesting and unique genetic variation in an established cultivar such as the unusually speckled bean whose seed he saved and which he has dubbed Marvel of Nictaux. He hopes to grow this new seed out again next year to stabilize it before offering it for sale to his customers.

One gets the sense, in talking to Owen, that his company is more of a vocation than purely a business. He often speaks of the importance of self-sufficiency, a philosophy he clearly lives himself—he and his family enjoy the bounty of the Annapolis Valley harvest growing literally in their own backyard. As for his customers, "Growing our own food is going to be a valuable skill in the future," he says.

Sebastian Margarit: Vista Bella Farm

A visit with Sebastian Margarit, owner of Vista Bella Farm in Malagash, dispels many popular misconceptions about farming on Nova Scotia's North Shore—and about farming generally. The first surprise in store for me at Vista Bella is Sebastian's small but sturdy crop of artichokes, an experiment, he tells me, that failed three times before he discovered the secret to growing these delectables in a climate vastly unlike their Mediterranean homeland: "I tricked them into thinking our early spring was really the mild winter they're used to." By planting them outside in early spring this year, Sebastian guaranteed his tender plants a full late spring and early summer's worth of growth and was able to bring them to market in July.

Sebastian is a graduate student at the Nova Scotia Agricultural College; his area of expertise is compost teas, and a small portion of his 26-hectare property is devoted to his research on the effects of different fertilizers on asparagus. He is a regular seller at the Truro Farmers' Market, about an hour's drive from home, where he lives with his partner, Brenna, and their two small sons. On my drive to the farm, I noticed a flourishing apple orchard next to the Margarit property and a roadside stand full of fruit. This is the second surprise of my visit: like many Nova Scotians, I'm sure, I once believed that the province's only productive orchards were located in the Annapolis Valley. Tramping along the deep tractor ruts on our way to his own substantial orchard, Sebastian assures me that this is not the case. In fact, "we actually get more sun in Malagash than in the Valley, but they get more heat." His two-year-old nectarine, pear, apple, and peach trees are arranged in rows along a sunny slope that leads down to Tatamagouche Bay; the ocean breezes here help to moderate the effects of an otherwise harsh North Shore winter. The heavy build-up of snow on the hillside insulates the fruit-tree roots against the cold. This same current of sea air leading to a later fall frost than in the province's interior is the secret of other farming success stories in the area, most notably the Jost Vineyards nearby.

The eclectic collection of vegetables grown at Vista Bella reflects many of Sebastian's personal tastes. "I tend to grow things I like because if it doesn't sell, I get to eat what I like to eat." Purple cauliflowers, teardrop-shaped cabbages, sweet potatoes, and a staggering assortment of eggplants are just some of the crops burgeoning in the fields and in the large greenhouse nearby. Predicting customer demand is often a tricky business for a small grower. "One week I picked three Rubbermaid containers of basil and sold only two bags. We ended up making pesto and freezing it for ourselves. It got so that

Sebastian Margarit in his greenhouse

Purple broccoli is loaded with antioxidants.

One of Sebastian's "Fairy Tale" eggplants

A tempting melon grown by Sebastian

even the smell of basil made me sick to my stomach." Once he discovered that his customers preferred potted basil plants rather than the cut herb, basil became a good seller at the market.

Sebastian is a strong believer in sustainable farming practices and in making healthy food available to all regardless of income, an ethos that sometimes puts him at odds with certified organic standards. While he doesn't use pesticides on any of his produce and calls himself "75 to 80 percent organic," some of the soil amendments he uses are not to be found on the list of acceptable organic products. The high price of certified organic food, according to Sebastian, creates "a two-tiered system of food that only a certain level of person can afford. I want to be able to feed single moms." Putting his words into action, Sebastian will fly to Alberta for the second time this year to teach community gardening and home preserving workshops to people living on reservations from the United States border to just south of the Northwest Territories. "Sustainability is where everything in agriculture should be directed," he says earnestly. Vista Bella Farm bears out that philosophy.

Michelle Smith: The tomato guru of Cape Breton Island

Cape Breton Island can be an unforgiving place in which to grow a vegetable garden—just ask Michelle Smith of Whycocomagh, who's been at it for more than twenty years. "In Cape Breton, we're very marginal for a lot of crops," she says ruefully, "especially the ones I love, unfortunately, like tomatoes, peppers, eggplants, and basil. It's extremely challenging and it's become more—or differently—challenging in the last ten years as we've seen the effects of climate change. But it was always tough to get a ripe tomato; that's why we make chow here in Cape Breton—the green ones are plentiful!"

Garden blends into pasture on Michelle Smith's farm.

A beautiful squash grown by Michelle

Michelle, a farmer who sells her produce and home-baked pies at the Mabou and Sydney farmers' markets, moved to Whycocomagh in 2006 from an established farm even farther north, near Cape Smokey; the three-hour daily school-bus commute to Baddeck was too much for her young son, Linden. Her daughter Rosie, a recent graduate of Mount Allison University with her mother's interest in plant biology and farming, now tends the first farm. The piece of land Michelle and Linden moved to, on a windy hillside in dairy-farm country near Mabou, didn't have a house on it, so they set about building one themselves. ("How many ten-year-olds get to design and build their own houses?" she laughs.) The Smith household and premises now include twelve sheep, one milk cow, two steers, a dog, and a cat. The animals are kept mainly for the manure they provide to fertilize Michelle's organic gardens, but their meat, milk, and fleece are also used by the family, making them nearly completely self-sufficient.

There is more to Michelle's vegetable gardens than just a food supply. "Largely what

Tomatoes planted in fish crates (or other containers) can easily be moved.

I do is save seed stock. My garden doesn't look like anybody else's; the tomatoes are in twenty-five different places, as are the beans, and I grow only one variety of each squash family per year [to prevent cross-pollination]. I've also started an open-pollinated onion project this year to see which varieties will do well in this climate and which I can collect seed from. It really looks like chaos, but there is order to it." In any given year, Michelle grows out and saves seed from twenty to twenty-five varieties of heritage tomatoes, some of them seldom grown nowadays. These rarities are given special treatment, spending the season in a local school's greenhouse. To keep the varieties she grows at home from crossing, Michelle plants her seed tomatoes in fish crates almost 8 metres (25 feet) apart from each other; these crates can be easily moved or brought indoors if an early frost threatens.

Partly through her involvement with Seeds of Diversity's tomato project, an attempt to germinate older varieties of tomato that had languished for fifty years in a government gene bank in Saskatoon, and partly through her local reputation as a sucker for a good tomato, Michelle has acquired several hundred varieties of her favourite vegetable. In spring, she offers a wide assortment of tomato transplants at the Sydney market, acting as match-maker for her customers and their produce. The sign at her table reads, "Match a tomato to your personality: free technical support all summer." Some of the questions she asks prospective buyers: "How much time and effort do you want to spend on the garden? How much space do you have? Are you willing to stake and/or provide a wire cage for the tomato plant? Is it windy in your yard? Are you looking for a sauce, salad, or sandwich-type tomato?"

Her obvious passion for plants and plant lore makes Michelle a natural and engaging teacher; she frequently gives talks and seminars at garden centres and schools around the province.

Several years of experience as a market grower in Ontario ("God's own climate for tomatoes," as she calls it) prior to moving to Cape Breton taught Michelle an important lesson about the highly variable Canadian climate and its effects on crops. "Those few years in Ontario I had no problems growing and ripening all kinds of hybrid tomatoes that were productive and disease-resistant. I learned that hybrid varieties that are designed for an ideal climate don't flourish in our short Cape Breton summers." Due in part to repeated failures of her hybrid tomato crop, Michelle started experimenting with hardier open-pollinated varieties, which she found to be more adaptable and better able to handle the stresses of increasingly chaotic summers that can swing from wet and cold to hot and dry in a short period. Additionally, these open-pollinated tomatoes—lovingly dubbed "mongrels" by Michelle—have the advantage of being less demanding on soil and able to tolerate marginal conditions. Michelle's tomato food mix also boosts her crop and includes crushed oyster shells (for calcium), Epsom salts (for magnesium), and wood ash (for potassium).

"I found that if I planted enough varieties, I was always going to get ripe tomatoes, no matter what kind of summer we had. Now, twenty years later, I've come to understand that that's how we really have to look at food security generally. The scattershot approach makes sure you've got *something* to eat."

In a world of monoculture-based farming, a single crop failure could spell disaster, something Michelle is all too aware of. "We didn't learn anything from the Irish potato famine; that was a long time ago and we're still doing the same thing: one variety, very productive, but it will be one virus that kills it and we won't have a backup."

While it is a sad reality that farmers everywhere are struggling to survive, even a short visit to any of our province's bustling farmers' markets will also reveal the encouraging recent surge in public support for local food providers (look for the telling bumper sticker seen on cars around Nova Scotia that reads "No Farms, No Food"). Local farmers deserve our undying gratitude for the hard work they do, and I wish I could write a chapter, if not a book, about each of them. For a paean to local growers, see Heliotrust's *Twilight Meetings: Celebrating the Wisdom of Our Farmer-Mentors*, published in 2007, a collection of essays on the lives and times of twenty-three Maritime farmers.

It's the last week of May as I write this, and I'm looking out the window at another rainy Nova Scotian day, wondering again if I planted my tomatoes too soon. The arugula and spinach I put in some weeks ago and have been enjoying in salads have now started to bolt; for some reason, the lettuce didn't amount to much this year. The slugs have already started chewing the comfrey, while the bees poke their heads into its tiny, violet flowers. Every year, I learn something new about my garden and its inhabitants; sometimes, it's the failures that teach the best lessons. A garden is a wonderful, humbling teacher.

My wishes for you as you embark on your own gardening adventure: a sense of wonder, a bit of patience, and the best of luck.

Selected Bibliography

(not even close to an exhaustive one...)

Composting, mulching, and soil amendments

Campbell, Stu. *Let It Rot! The Gardener's Guide to Composting. (*North Adams, MA: Storey Publishing, 1998).

Dunne, Niall, ed. *Healthy Soils for Sustainable Gardens.* (Brooklyn: Brooklyn Botanic Garden, 2009).

Stout, Ruth. *The No-Work Garden Book.* (Emmaus, PA: Rodale Press, 1971).

Growing in small spaces

Bird, Christopher. *Cubed Foot Gardening: Growing Vegetables in Raised, Intensive Beds.* (Guilford, CT: The Lyons Press, 2001).

Guerra, Michael. *The Edible Container Garden: Growing Fresh Food in Small Places.* (New York: Fireside/Simon and Schuster, 2000).

Logan, Eileen. *How To Grow Organic Vegetables in Containers…Anywhere.* (New York: Writers Club Press, 2002).

Rees, Yvonne. *The Art of Balcony Gardening.* (London: Ward Lock, 1991).

Urban and suburban vegetable gardening

Ball, Jeff. *The Self-Sufficient Suburban Garden.* (Emmaus, PA: Rodale Press, 1983).

Bennett, Jennifer. *The New Northern Gardener.* (Willowdale, ON: Firefly Books, 1996).

Coyne, Kelly, and Erik Knutzen. *The Urban Homestead.* (Port Townsend, WA: Process Media, 2008).

SPIN farming webpage: spinfarming.com

Lead in garden soil

Canadian Council of Ministers of the Environment. *Canadian Soil Quality Guidelines for the Protection of Environmental and Human Health: Lead.* 1999. Canadian Council of Ministers of the Environment: http://www.ceqg-rcqe.ccme.ca/download/en/269.

Rosen, Carl J. "Lead in the Home Garden and Urban Soil Environment." University of Minnesota Extension Service: http://www.extension.umn.edu/distribution/horticulture/DG2543.html, 2002.

Seed saving

Apple, H., D. Joubert, and B. Wildfong, eds. *How To Save Your Own Seeds.* (Toronto: Seeds of Diversity, 2005).* (A French version of this book is also available.)

Turner, Carole. *Seed Sowing and Saving.* (Pownal, Vermont: Storey Communications, Inc., 1998).

General information/vegetable lore and recipes

The Encyclopaedia Britannica: Macropaedia.
15th ed. 1983, s.v. "vegetables and vegetable farming."

Atlas, Nava. *Vegetariana.* (Garden City: The Dial Press/Doubleday, 1984).

Beliveau, Richard, and Denis Gingras. *Cooking With Foods That Fight Cancer.* (Toronto: McClelland and Stewart, 2007).

Robertson, Laurel, Carol Flinders, and Bronwen Godfrey. *Laurel's Kitchen.* (New York: Bantam Press, 1978). * (A more recent edition is *The New Laurel's Kitchen*, Ten Speed Press, 1986.)

Wells, Troth. *The World in Your Kitchen.* (Oxford: The New Internationalist Publications Ltd, 1988).

Weeds: identification and uses

Szczawinski, Adam, and Nancy Turner. *Edible Garden Weeds Of Canada.* (Ottawa: National Museums of Canada, 1978).

Preserving the harvest

Bubel, Mike, and Nancy Bubel. *Root Cellaring: The Simple No-Processing Way To Store Fruits and Vegetables.* (Pownal, Vermont: Storey Communications, 1991).

Greene, Janet, Ruth Hertzberg, and Beatrice Vaughan. *Putting Food By,* 4th ed. (Lexington, MA: The Stephen Greene Press, 1988).

Portland Preserve, http://www.portlandpreserve.com (A very helpful website on home preserving methods based in Oregon and run by Harriet Fasenfest.)

Companion planting/Shade tolerance in plants

Riotte, Louise. *Carrots Love Tomatoes.* (Pownal, Vermont: Storey Communications, 1975).

Riotte, Louise. *Roses Love Garlic: Secrets of Companion Planting With Flowers.* (Pownal, Vermont: Garden Way Publishing, 1983).

Old House Interiors magazine, http://www.oldhouseweb.com/gardening/vegetables-shade.shtml

Growing vegetables in Nova Scotia

Major, Marjorie. *From the Ground: The Story of Planting in Nova Scotia.* (Halifax: Petheric Press, 1981).

Willison, Marjorie. *East Coast Gardener: A Month-by-Month Guide to Successful Gardening.* (Halifax: Nimbus, 2006).

Inspirational reading

Coleman, Eliot. *The New Organic Grower's Four-Season Harvest.* (Camden East, ON: Old Bridge Press, 1992).

Flores, H. C. *Food Not Lawns: How To Turn Your Yard Into a Garden And Your Neighborhood Into A Community.* (White River Junction, VT: Chelsea Green Publishing Company, 2006).

Heliotrust. *Twilight Meetings: Celebrating the Wisdom of Our Farmer-Mentors* (The Avondale Press, 2007)

Kingsolver, Barbara. *Animal, Vegetable, Miracle.* (Toronto: Harper Perennial, 2008).

Other resources for individual vegetable histories and properties

Food Reference Website, http://www.foodreference.com

Health Care Clinic, http://www.health-care-clinic.org

The *Food History* website, http://www.kitchenproject.com

The British Potato Council website, http://www.potato.org.uk

The World Carrot Museum website, http://www.carrotmuseum.co.uk

Image Credits

Index

Depending on the season, Elizabeth Peirce is a writer
and gardener who lives in Halifax, Nova Scotia. She
has worked in vegetable gardens since she was old
enough to hold a watering can and is passionate
about local food and food security issues. She is
the author and co-author of two previous books:
*Saladin: Piracy, Mutiny and Murder On the High
Seas,* and *The Pirate Rebel.*